CAPTAIN COOK
Explores the Pacific in World History

Ann Graham Gaines

Enslow Publishers, Inc.

40 Industrial Road   PO Box 38
Box 398   Aldershot
Berkeley Heights, NJ 07922   Hants GU12 6BP
USA   UK

http://www.enslow.com

Library of Congress Cataloging-in-Publication Data

Gaines, Ann Graham
    Captain Cook explores the Pacific in world history / Ann Graham
Gaines.
        p. cm. — (In world history)
    Includes bibliographical references (p.) and index.
    ISBN 0-7660-1823-7
    1. Cook, James, 1728–1779—Journeys—Juvenile literature. 2.
Explorers—England—Biography—Juvenile literature. 3. Voyages around
the world—Juvenile literature. 4. Oceania—Discovery and exploration—
Juvenile literature. [1. Cook, James, 1728–1779. 2. Explorers. 3. Voyages
around the world.] I. Title. II. Series.
        G420.C65 G35 2002
        910′.92—dc21

                                                            2001001696

Printed in the United States of America

10 9 8 7 6 5 4 3 2 1

To Our Readers: We have done our best to make sure all Internet addresses in
this book were active and appropriate when we went to press. However, the
author and the publisher have no control over and assume no liability for the
material available on those Internet sites or on other Web sites they may link to.
Any comments or suggestions can be sent by e-mail to comments@enslow.com or
to the address on the back cover.

Illustration Credits: Drawing by John Webber, engraving by Benjamin
Thomas Pouncy, p. 97; Drawing by John Webber, engraving by Charles Grignion,
p. 16; Drawing by John Webber, engraving by Francesco Bartolozzi (figures) and
William Byrne (landscape), p. 100; Drawing by John Webber, engraving by John
Hall, p. 88; Drawing by John Webber, engraving by John Hall (figures) and
Samuel Middiman (landscape), p. 91; Drawing by John Webber, engraving by
John Keyse Sherwin, pp. 57, 110; Drawing by John Webber, engraving by Thomas
Cook, p. 113; Drawing by John Webber, engraving by William Byrne, p. 107;
Drawing by John Webber, engraving by William Sharp, pp. 92, 101; Enslow
Publishers, Inc., pp. 4, 7, 11, 63, 95; Library of Congress, pp. 27, 38, 48.

Cover Illustration: The Albert and Shirley Small Special Collections Library,
University of Virginia Library (Background Map); Library of Congress (Cook
Portrait)

Contents

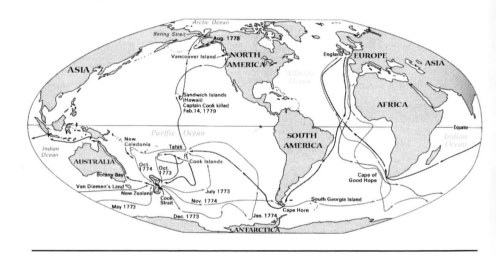

A map of Cook's many journeys.

Chapter 1

James Cook "Discovers" Hawaii

On January 18, 1778, explorer James Cook, commander of two British ships, was in the middle of the Pacific Ocean. He was headed for the northwest coast of North America, which was still thousands of miles away. Suddenly, at daybreak, he was utterly amazed, as he wrote, when "an island made its appearance, and soon after we saw more land entirely detached from the former."[1] For days, Cook had known that land was nearby, because he had seen seabirds. But he knew that finding that land was unlikely—it could lie in any direction and be hundreds of miles away. Nor did he expect that it would be worth finding, anyway. His last landfall, some three weeks earlier, had been on what he had named Christmas Island. This was a barren, uninhabited atoll, or outcrop of coral, with no fresh water and, therefore, no plants or land animals. But even from a distance, these new islands appeared green and lush. The intrepid explorer had become the first European known to have seen Hawaii.

Cook sailed on. The next morning, he sighted a third island, "as far distant as land could be seen."[2] Soon, canoes were approaching from the shore. He ordered his ships to slow so he could meet the native people in the canoes. As soon as the paddlers shouted greetings, Cook realized that they spoke a language related to that of Tahiti. Having already spent months in Tahiti and other Polynesian islands, he was able to communicate with them. Wanting to make a friendly gesture, Cook lowered to one canoe a rope on which he had tied brass medals. His gift caused great excitement. The natives gave him fruit and fish in return.

Realizing that he had found a beautiful, rich new land with friendly people, Cook decided to look for a place to land on the island the natives called Kauai (which it is still called today). As he coasted to the shore, more canoes were put into the water. Men, women, and children also swam out to the ships, so curious were they to see the newcomers. Cook saw many more natives on the beaches, looking out at his ships. The sailors continued to trade with the natives in the canoes, exchanging nails for pigs and sweet potatoes. Cook allowed a few natives to come on board his ship. The islanders said they had never before seen sailing ships with great white sails on tall masts. They were fascinated with the Englishmen's fair skin and blond, red, or brown hair.

Finally, Cook found a safe bay. Anchoring, he could see a village on the shore. Small boats were lowered to take Cook and his crew to shore. Cook leaped into the first and headed for the beach. Several hundred natives had gathered there. When Cook stepped out of the lead boat onto the sand, he later wrote, "all fell flat on their faces, and remained in that humble posture till . . . [I] made signs to them to rise."[3] Later, he discovered that this was how the native people welcomed all high-ranking chiefs. Clearly, they considered Cook an important man.

A view of Cook's ships arriving at port in Hawaii.

Then they honored him with a ceremony. They presented Cook with "a great many small pigs" and fronds from local trees. A native then delivered what seemed to be a long prayer. Cook wrote, "I expressed my acceptance of their proffered friendship by giving them in return such presents as I had brought with me from the ship for that purpose."[4]

The next two weeks were happy times for Cook and his men. The sailors were used to spending many weeks at a time on board their ships. Voyages were dangerous. Sometimes storms broke and the crew members had all they could do just to keep the vessels afloat. But mostly, the sailors' days were filled with monotonous hard work. They were glad to spend time on this tropical island, with its beautiful beaches, pigs to barbecue, fruit to pick, and women to romance.

Captain Cook did not relax with his men, but he enjoyed himself nevertheless. Three times, he went far inland. There, he saw a temple and well-tended plantations where taro—a tasty root vegetable—was grown.[5] Everywhere he went he met friendly natives. He found them very likable people and marveled over their carvings, their bark cloth, and their cloaks and caps "upon which the most beautiful red and yellow feathers are so closely fixed, that the surface might be compared to the thickest and richest velvet . . ."[6] Cook discovered that the natives already had a few iron objects. He wondered whether this meant that Spanish ships had already been there. Eventually, though, he concluded that the natives had removed the iron from driftwood from shipwrecks that had washed up on their beaches.[7] He described everything he saw in his journal and collected examples of their craftsmanship.

When rain and winds brought high seas, Cook moved his ships out of the harbor. Then he found a safer haven, on the nearby island of Niihau. There, he was also greeted with great ceremony by the natives. Once again, he was awarded the respect usually reserved for high chiefs.

Had he not had a family waiting at home in England and a mission to fulfill, Cook would have been pleased to spend the rest of his life in Hawaii. He knew that time was of the essence, however. He had orders to reach the northwest coast of North America by summer. King George III of England wanted him to search for the west end of the fabled Northwest Passage, the water course from the Atlantic Ocean to the Pacific Ocean. Thus, on February 2, 1778, Cook left Hawaii. But he hoped to return one day.

Chapter 2

The South Pacific Before Cook's Arrival

It was not until James Cook began his explorations that Europeans began to learn about the Pacific Ocean, its thousands of islands, and the people who lived on them.

The Pacific Ocean covers an area of 69.4 million square miles. At its widest point, it stretches about 12,300 miles from Indonesia to the coast of Colombia. The lowest known point on Earth, the Marianas Trench, is in the Pacific. It was named "Pacific" by Ferdinand Magellan during his trip around the globe in 1519–1522.

The Pacific Ocean is largely empty. It has just three major land masses: Australia, New Guinea, and New Zealand. The northern Pacific is empty, as is the ocean in the area west of North and South America. There are about twenty-five thousand islands south of

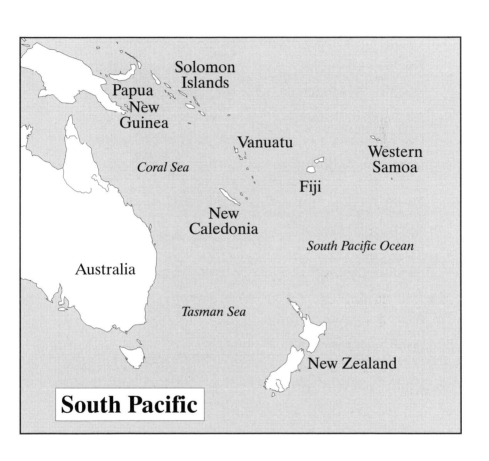

The South Pacific holds thousands of islands, both large and small.

the equator. New islands still appear from time to time. Others, which stood just a few feet above sea level earlier, sometimes disappear. Some small, isolated Pacific islands are not inhabited.

Geographers separate the Pacific Islands into four groups: the Philippines and Indonesia, Micronesia, Melanesia, and Polynesia.[1] The islands of Indonesia and Melanesia are large and close set. Micronesia and Polynesia include many smaller islands, set farther apart. Islands in the Pacific come in three types: continental islands, which were formed when land broke off from a continent; high islands, which arise from volcanic activity; and coral islands.

Polynesia

The islands of Polynesia, where Cook made his historic discoveries, cover a huge territory in the middle of the Pacific Ocean. Polynesia includes all the islands that are found within the triangle formed by the Hawaiian islands, Easter Island, and New Zealand. Inside the triangle are several large groups of islands, including the Hawaiian Islands, the Cook Islands, the Marquesas, the Tuamotu Archipelago, and the Society Islands. Also part of Polynesia are Samoa, Tokelau, and Tonga.

The islands of Polynesia are sometimes called the South Sea islands. The high islands were formed when ancient volcanoes spewed forth basalt, a hard, dense, dark rock. The Hawaiian, Society, and Samoan Islands have high mountains. Inland, waterfalls cascade in their deep gorges, or valleys. Beautiful beaches edge these islands, which are protected by barrier reefs, long ridges of coral that form along coastlines. Calm lagoons separate the barrier reefs from the coastlines. The climate of the South Pacific is tropical. Hot temperatures and frequent rain encourage lush vegetation on many of the islands. Fruit and flowers abound. This is not true, however, on atolls, which are formed of coral. Rising just a few feet above sea level, these atolls are often devastated by hurricanes.

As amazing as it seems, given the distance between these far-flung islands, all their native peoples belong to the same ethnic group. They descend from the same ancestors. As a group, they are known as Polynesians. Five hundred years ago, Polynesians were "the most widely spread people on earth."[2] They had been so for three thousand years. They stretched across an area twice as wide as the continental United States. In that area, the ratio of water to land is approximately seventy to one.

Settlement

Historians do not know for sure how Polynesia was settled. There is debate as to where the first Polynesians came from. Some speculate the first settlers came from South America. In 1947, Norwegian explorer and ethnologist Thor Heyerdahl tried to prove this by sailing west from Callao, Peru, on a balsa raft called *Kon-Tiki*. He and his crew reached Raroia in the Tuamotu Archipelago, located in the southern

Pacific east of Tahiti, after 101 days. They used just wind and currents. Today, most scholars believe Polynesians' ancestors came from the Philippines and eastern Indonesia. Melanesians—people from the islands northeast of Australia and south of the equator (including the Solomons, New Hebrides, and New Caledonia)—expanded into Polynesia later, from 1600 to 1000 B.C.

There has been a great deal of research into ancient voyages in the Pacific. Some research has been undertaken by historians and some by scientists. To learn more about how and why ancient people ventured out onto the ocean in boats, scholars have studied Polynesian migration myths. Some provide information about navigation techniques.[3] Scholars have also gone to the islands to observe the traditional methods of navigation that some Polynesians still use today. In the Carolina islands, sailors can still learn to make a star compass out of pebbles. Some scholars have even recreated early voyages.[4]

Scholar Brian Durrans studies how early European explorers like Cook *thought* the Polynesians traveled from one island to the next.[5] In 1722, Dutch explorer Jacob Roggeven had already asked himself how people got to the islands in the Pacific. He did not understand the span of the ocean, but he realized that the islands were at least hundreds of miles from South America, New Guinea, and Australia. He wondered whether the people living there had migrated from island to island or whether God had simply created them where they lived, as most people of the time believed.

Cook knew that Polynesians traveled from island to island. He met natives on one island who had been born elsewhere. He also heard many voyagers' stories. He was impressed with the length of their trips and how often they attempted voyages. He also recorded examples of "drift" voyages, made by mistake, such as those made by fishermen who were caught at sea during a storm.[6] Cook also noticed the degree to which customs were shared from island to island.

Cook himself had learned to navigate by the stars and by dead reckoning (using clues besides the stars), as was required in the variable weather around Great Britain. One reason he thought the South Pacific natives might do the same is because mistakenly he believed there was a chain of islands stretching from Polynesia to the East Indies, each just a few hundred leagues—a measurement equivalent to three miles—apart.[7] Other thinkers believed a sunken continent existed in the Pacific from which island settlement had occurred.[8] Archaeologists' finds show that a prehistoric trade system carried goods more than a thousand miles.[9]

Long voyages were made in outrigger canoes. They were more stable than single canoes and suitable for long voyages and stormy weather. These remarkable vessels could carry people, plants, and animals hundreds of miles. Early navigators introduced coconut, taro (a big, edible tuber sweeter than a potato), yam,

Hawaiian canoes measured twenty-four feet in length and only fifteen inches in width. Often the Hawaiians built double canoes. Single narrow canoes had to have an outrigger for balance.

banana, breadfruit, and pigs, dogs, and chickens to various islands.[10]

Archaeologists believe that Java, a large island in the western Pacific, was the first South Pacific island settled by human beings. Australia and New Guinea were probably settled forty thousand years ago. It took many thousands of years for people to reach the smaller Pacific islands. The first settlement in Polynesia was probably of the Tongan Islands. It had probably taken place by 1300 B.C. Melanesia, Micronesia, and Polynesia were completely settled by A.D. 1000.[11]

Peoples of the South Pacific

Once settlement was completed, the Polynesian civilization spread across half the Pacific. The ocean continued to play an important part in the life of the people. In areas where islands lay close together, people used canoes to travel from one island to another to trade or visit friends or relatives. They also went out onto the ocean to hunt and fish. All Polynesians ate a great deal of fish and other marine animals, such as turtles. Trees provided fruit, including mangoes, coconuts, papayas, and bananas, and taro and sweet potatoes grew on many islands. In many cases, Polynesians grew their own plants for food.

People on each island developed their own traditions, although lifestyles throughout Polynesia remained similar. Even though the islands of Polynesia spread out over a great distance, their people spoke related languages. Some words closely resembled each other. This was especially true of words for plants and animals. Polynesians spoke about thirty interrelated languages by the eighteenth century. Polynesian languages all belong to the Austronesian family. The total number of people who spoke a Polynesian language was between three hundred thousand and four hundred thousand in 1770.[12] No Polynesian people had a written language.

Across Polynesia, people lived in simple houses. Often they had stone floors, wood walls, and thatched roofs. Extended families often lived very close together. In general, Polynesians did not live in towns or villages. They built their homesteads some distance apart from others. Around their homesteads they grew crops. Most settlements were located on an island's coast or in fertile valleys.

Polynesian people were organized into tribes or chiefdoms. Tribes were ruled by chiefs. Generally, chiefs inherited their position. When a chief died, his son would become chief.[13] Chiefs controlled land distribution, deciding who would live where. Often, tribes fought over land. Powerful rulers demanded tribute—payments that could take the form of goods or services—from less powerful people.

All across Polynesia, the people worshipped similar gods and had similar religious ceremonies. In essence, they worshipped nature. Chiefs were believed to have mystical power. Tradition and custom dictated that some behavior was considered *tapu,* or taboo. That meant these behaviors were considered wrong by the society. In Polynesia, taboo kept people from using, approaching, or mentioning certain topics or places.

Today, anthropologists divide Polynesia into two cultural divisions: eastern and western Polynesia. In both, the traditional lifestyle was similar, but there were distinctions in the particular types of weapons and fishhooks used and in the carvings the people made. The two groups also differed in the way they made bark cloth; built houses, temples, and canoes; regarded kinship; and practiced religion.

Hawaii

The most important Polynesian cultures James Cook encountered were those of Hawaii, the Society Islands, and New Zealand.

In Cook's day, eight of the 122 Hawaiian islands were inhabited. Anthropologists believe the islands were inhabited by A.D. 500. The first settlers probably came from the Marquesas, islands two thousand miles south and east of Hawaii.

The Hawaiians had a stratified, or layered, society. It included four separate classes of people. Social rank was very important to Hawaiians. The highest-ranking were chiefs and nobles, whom Hawaiians believed were descended from gods. Priests and craftsmen made up the second class. Commoners—farmers and fishermen—formed a third class. The lowest class was made up of slaves and outcasts. Sometimes one chiefdom captured members of another, making these people slaves. At other times, people were thrown out of one chiefdom and they went to live with another group. These were outcasts.

Religious laws governed the society. Chiefs were both government and religious officials. Major Hawaiian gods included Kane, the creator of nature and men; Tu, the god of war; and Rongo, god of horticulture. The gods were worshipped at open-air temples. Each temple included an oracle tower, where priests went to receive messages from the gods. Once a year, Hawaiians celebrated at *makahiki*, a harvest festival. No one was allowed to work or fight during the first period of *makahiki*. During this first period, everyone brought their taxes to the temples. During a second period of the festival, the people held great feasts.

Hawaiians lived in villages rather than on scattered homesteads like many Polynesian peoples. Wooden frames supported their buildings' thatched roofs and walls. The men cooked, while women raised the children and did crafts, making clothing and other things people needed in their everyday lives. Males and females ate separately. They wore clothing of decorated bark cloth and leis, or necklaces, of shell, seeds, ivory, or feathers. Chiefs wore elaborate costumes to ceremonies. Their costumes included cloaks, capes, and helmets covered with feathers.

When wars broke out between members of different chiefdoms on the Islands, as was often the case, chiefs paid soldiers to fight for them. In their free time, Hawaiians danced, sang, and played games.[14]

The Society Islands

The two groups of islands that lie between the equator and the Tropic of Capricorn in the Pacific Ocean are called the Society Islands. To the east lie the Windward group. To the west lie the Leeward group.

When Cook saw the Society Islands in the 1760s, a total of seventy thousand people lived there. Anthropologists believe their ancestors came from

Asia, perhaps around the South China Sea. The islands may have been settled as early as A.D. 650.

Like other Polynesians, the people who inhabited the Society Islands believed the universe was created by the god Ta'aroa. They also believed that gods and humans interacted. The people worshiped at open-air temples called *marae.*

Society was divided into three classes. The aristocracy—or chiefs and nobles—ranked highest. The middle class was called the *ra'atira.* The *manahune,* or commoners, cultivated the land. Class was determined by genealogy, or ancestry. In other words, people inherited their position in society.

Chiefs were in charge of dividing up the land. Different chiefdoms competed constantly for territory and prestige, leading to frequent wars. Many battles were fought on the water in canoes.

When Cook arrived, the people of the Society Islands lived on scattered homesteads. They built their houses of wood. Their roofs were thatch. They had few furnishings. The people fished and farmed for food. The staple of their diet was breadfruit, a large round yellow fruit that grows on an evergreen tree. They raised pigs, dogs, and birds to eat.

Society Island men and women oiled their hair and wore many earrings made of shells, seeds, or pearls. They put flowers in their hair. They tattooed their bodies. Overweight people with fair skin were considered most attractive. Marriages were not considered permanent—men and women could have children with several different people.

The Society Islanders had plenty of free time. They spent many days visiting friends and relations and playing sports. They liked to swim, surf, wrestle, and box.[15]

New Zealand

New Zealand's native peoples are called the Maori. Anthropologists believe their ancestors probably came from Tahiti around A.D. 750. According to Maori folklore, however, they arrived around 1350 in what translates as the Great Fleet. The Great Fleet was made up of hundreds of canoes carrying not just humans, but plants and dogs.

In the eighteenth century, Maori society was organized into tribes. Each tribe traced its lineage from a different member of the Great Fleet crews. In the 1760s, people lived in large households, headed by old men. As in the Society Islands, genealogy dictated one's social status. The Maori kept slaves, usually people captured in war.

The people lived in fortified villages. Fences surrounded the villages, which usually sat on hills. A large open space sat in the middle of each village. There, villagers could gather for feasts and meetings. Houses had wood frames and thatched sides. Because the climate is colder than in Hawaii or the Society Islands, the houses contained fire pits where fires could be built during the winter.

The Maori tribes fought constantly. Often, wars broke out between different tribes over insults to individual members. Other wars were fought for retribution. Every able-bodied man trained as a warrior. Warriors ate some of those people they killed in battle. It was considered even more disgraceful for a warrior to be captured and enslaved than to be killed.

The Maori grew sweet potatoes, taro, and yams to eat. They also foraged for fern root. They fished and trapped or hunted birds.

The Maori used their fingers to weave the fibers of a flax-like plant into cloaks and kilts. They also wore tattoos and earrings. The Maori were fine wood-carvers who elaborately decorated their boats, paddles, walking sticks, bowls, and flutes. They built very big canoes. Some could carry a hundred men. At one end, the canoe featured a carved figure.[16]

Contact

As James Cook discovered, the peoples of the South Pacific did not know about all the other peoples who lived in that vast expanse of ocean. But through voyaging, people from different islands did come into contact with one another.

In general, however, by the time James Cook began his voyages, they had not yet come into contact with Europeans. This first contact would affect the native peoples of the South Pacific greatly, mostly in negative ways.

Chapter 3

Early Explorers of the Pacific

In the 1760s, much of the Pacific Ocean remained unexplored by Europeans. But world maps did not leave the region blank. Included on maps of the time was a continent that was believed to exist, even though it had not yet been seen. Sometimes it was labeled Terra Australis Incognita, the unknown southern land. Other maps called it Terra Australis Nondum Incognita, the southern land not yet known.

Europeans' belief in this continent went back more than a thousand years. From ancient times, philosophers believed that land must be evenly distributed around the globe. Otherwise, they thought the earth would be unbalanced and would "topple to destruction amidst the stars."[1] Realizing how much of the Northern Hemisphere is land, they thought the same must be true south of the equator. Greek geographer Ptolemy

Source Document

Hawai'i Loa, or Ke Kowa i Hawai'i, was one of the four children of Aniani Ka Lani. The other three were Ki, who settled in Tahiti, Kana Loa, who settled the Marquesas, and Laa-Kapu. . . . Only two islands existed and both were discovered and settled by Hawai'i Loa. The first he named Hawai'i after himself, the second Maui, after his eldest son. . . . Hawai'i Loa was a distinguished man and noted for his fishing excursions which would occupy months. . . . Once when they had been at sea for a long time, Makali'i, the principal navigator said to Hawai'i Loa, "Let's steer the canoe in the direction of Iao, the Eastern Star. . . . There is land to the eastward. . . ." So they steered straight onward and arrived at the easternmost island of the Hawaiian chain.[2]

The native Hawaiian people told this tale of how their land was discovered by a man named Hawai'i Loa.

suggested that one great southern continent must exist. Europeans looked forward to the day it would be found. Explorers searched for it. Kings gladly paid for their voyages, since this unknown continent was fabled to be a land of great beauty and fabulous riches.

Polynesians had explored much of the Pacific Ocean before the Europeans arrived. Travel from east to west was easiest because of the winds and ocean currents. According to Hawaiian oral history, Hawaii-Loa, who discovered Hawaii, was the first recorded Polynesian explorer. But for many years, the area remained unexplored by Europeans.

European Voyages

During the so-called First Great Age of Exploration— from the late 1300s, when the Portuguese started to search for new routes to the Far East, to 1768, when James Cook started his first voyage—Portugal, Spain, the Netherlands, England, and France sent out explorers to "explore, discover, and usually conquer" the rest of the world.[3] During this period, the kings and queens of these countries were eager to gain wealth. If their ships could sail to the Orient, they were sure to profit: The East had goods such as spices and silk that were in great demand in Europe.

Finding new trade routes to the Far East was only one reason explorers set out. Monarchs also gave them money for voyages, hoping they would find new lands to claim. Interest in building empires grew. In many cases, the rulers' enthusiasm spilled over to their people, who took great pride in explorers' exploits. As knowledge spread during the period known as the Renaissance, thinkers all over Europe expressed more interest in "what lay beyond the boundaries of the known world."[4]

After Christopher Columbus returned to Spain from his voyage to the islands of the Caribbean Sea, he was sent twice more to the New World. There, he established a settlement on the island of Hispaniola. Over the following years, Spanish conquistadors (explorers who set out to conquer the lands they discovered) colonized Mexico, and then made further expeditions into

Christopher Columbus's visits to the Caribbean sparked a wave of interest in New World exploration. Queen Isabella of Spain (sitting at left) listens as Columbus (standing at right) speaks.

Central, North, and South America. They were always searching for riches. In 1513, Vasco Núñez de Balboa became the first European to see the Pacific Ocean from North America when he explored Panama.

The establishment of a European presence in the Americas did not end the European interest in the Orient, however. On behalf of Portugal's King Manuel I, Vasco da Gama sailed from Lisbon south and east around Africa's Cape of Good Hope in 1497. On May 18, 1498, he reached India. From India, the Portuguese continued to sail east through the Indian Ocean. They encountered Indonesia, a group of islands in the Malay Archipelago off southeast Asia, and the Molucca Islands in 1513. Some historians speculate that they may have reached Australia.[5] But because the Portuguese king did not want competitors in the lucrative spice trade, he forbade da Gama and his crew to share their knowledge with people from other European countries—on pain of death. They were not even allowed to make maps showing the areas they had seen.

Magellan

Portuguese explorer Ferdinand Magellan was the captain of the first expedition known to sail around the world. In 1505, he sailed to India, with Francisco de Almeida, who had been appointed viceroy of the Indies by King Manuel I. From India, he traveled east as far as the Strait of Malacca, a channel that runs between Sumatra and the Malay Peninsula, connecting the Andaman Sea to the South China Sea. His king praised Magellan after he helped defend the Portuguese fort of Goa from 1507 to 1510 when it came under repeated attacks from pirates.

Then Magellan went to Morocco to fight a war Portugal was waging there against the Moors (Muslims from Africa and the Middle East). Soon, the king of Portugal accused Magellan of corruption, claiming Magellan was trading with captive Moors in order to make money for himself. The charges were never proven, but Magellan decided it was best to offer his services elsewhere.

The king of Spain agreed to sponsor Magellan in his own expedition, which began in 1519. Its purpose was to see if it might be possible to reach the Orient by rounding the tip of South America. Magellan's fleet of four ships became the first to round Cape Horn at the tip of South America in October 1520. He sailed through what is now known as the Strait of Magellan, which separates the tip of the continent of South America from the islands to the south. He and his crew made their first landfall on Guam in March 1521. By May, they had reached the Philippines. Magellan was killed there. One of his ships, carrying just 18 of the 230 men who had started out, finally limped back into harbor in Spain in September 1522.[6]

After Magellan

Portugal and Spain continued to compete as world explorers throughout the sixteenth century. In 1567, the Spanish viceroy, or governor, of Peru, land claimed by Spain, sent his nephew, Alvaro de Mendana de Neyra, to search for Terra Australis, the fabled southern continent. Mendana sailed through Polynesia but sighted just one atoll.

A new player then emerged on the scene. In 1578, Elizabeth I, the queen of England, sent Francis Drake on a search for Terra Australis. The voyage failed to find land, but it marked England's arrival as one of the major exploring powers.

Spain continued for a time to try to expand its empire and prevent England from making inroads. When the Spanish viceroy of Peru heard rumors that the rich Terra Australis lay to the west, he sent out an expedition from Callao, Peru. The expedition reached the Solomon Islands, north and east of Australia. The Spanish followed this voyage with an expedition that "discovered" New Guinea, which they recognized as a very large island. This, however, was the end of Spanish exploration of the Pacific. The government had decided not to spend any more money on searching for the unknown continent. It preferred to devote its funds to developing the colonies it had established already in the Americas.

By this time, the Netherlands had united to become a rich and powerful nation. The Dutch were extremely interested in the spice trade and the Orient. Searching for new places to trade, Dutch ship captains became the first Europeans to encounter Australia.

Other seafarers sighted the land, too. In 1627, a Dutch sea captain reached the south coast of

Australia, which the Dutch called New Holland. They mistakenly believed it to be a barren land inhabited by hostile people. Abel Tasman, another Dutch explorer, made historic voyages of discovery around the Australian continent. He also found the Fiji Islands, where he almost wrecked his ship. Tasman died in 1659. With his death, Dutch exploration efforts in the Pacific ended. By this time, several pieces of land—Australia, Java, Tierra del Fuego—had been charted as the fabled southern continent. They were later accepted as islands.[7]

By 1700, Europeans knew that there was one big landmass, Australia, in the Southern Hemisphere. But they expected to discover more new lands. They still thought that the Southern Hemisphere should contain more land than water, as in the Northern Hemisphere. Great stretches of the ocean were known. The Spanish and Dutch explorers' findings had made much smaller the area where a huge continent might lie.[8] But there still remained more to explore.

British Exploration

The British concentrated on settling North America in the seventeenth century. But in the eighteenth century, Great Britain's ambitions expanded. The English started to explore the Pacific Ocean, hoping to find the southern continent and claim it. John Byron sailed around the entire globe, but he did not locate a southern continent. Samuel Wallis undertook a new expedition to search for it. He circumnavigated the globe also, but could not find it, either. His countrymen were amazed, nonetheless, by his descriptions of Tahiti, the tropical island he was the first European to visit.

In 1767, Alexander Dalrymple, who lived in London, England, published a book about what explorers had learned so far about the South Pacific. There remained doubts and disputes concerning islands of the South Pacific. The east coast of Australia remained unknown, and the two islands of New Zealand were thought to be one. He discussed the proportion of land to water in the Northern Hemisphere. He believed this "[showed] that there is a seeming necessity for a Southern Continent."[9] He wrongly believed that early voyages had glimpsed the eastern coast of the legendary continent. He speculated that New Zealand was its west coast. In 1772, Dalrymple told the British government that there must be a Terra Australis Incognita or Isla Grande and that it would be in Great Britain's interest to find it. He described it in detail, saying "[this island] cannot fail of being a very temperate and pleasant Country, in a situation very favourable for carrying on the whale and other Fisheries, and also for the prosecution of any Commerce which may be found in the Countries to the South."[10] Now the race was on for Great Britain to explore the mysterious South Pacific.

Chapter 4

James Cook's Early Life

James Cook would become the British explorer to make the greatest explorations of the Pacific Ocean. When he was born, Great Britain was a very rich and powerful country. With its North American colonies, it had begun to build an empire. Great Britain would be one of the first nations to become industrialized, building factories where goods were manufactured. It also profited from trade, which its officials hoped to extend around the globe. Home to some of the world's greatest universities, Great Britain prided itself on its intellectual capabilities. In the eighteenth century, many notable thinkers and scientists lived there, people who were interested in learning all they could about the world and how it worked.

Cook's Youth

One day, Cook would make it possible for the British Empire to expand, while also collecting information that would astound scientists. Yet he came from humble beginnings. He was born on October 27, 1728, in a village named Marton-in-Cleveland, in Yorkshire, England. The village is located about fifteen miles from the North Sea, the body of water that separates England from Scandinavia. The area was mainly devoted to farming.

Cook's father was also named James. The elder James Cook had been born in Scotland in 1694. No record remains of why he decided to move to England or when he did so. Around 1715, many Scotsmen were emigrating because of political trouble in Scotland. Some Scotsmen wanted to place a rival to the current king on the British throne. These rebels tormented those who disagreed with their political beliefs. Other Scotsmen, however, went to England not to escape persecution, but to look for work.

As a young man, the elder James Cook had little education and few job skills. But even at age twenty, he was a serious, sober, hard-working man. He had little trouble persuading a farmer in Stainton-in-Cleveland in Yorkshire to hire him as a manual laborer.

In Stainton, James Cook met a young woman named Grace Pace. Her character was much like his. She was a quiet woman who was used to hard work and a simple life. They were married in 1725.

In 1726, their first child was born, a boy named John. Soon after, James, Grace, and John Cook moved to Marton-in-Cleveland, a few miles from

Stainton. There, they lived in a tiny, two-room cottage. It was made of clay and roofed with thatch.

Six other children were born to the Cooks. Only two, however, would live to adulthood. In the eighteenth century, it was common for children to die young, the victims of disease. James Cook, the future explorer, was born on October 27, 1728. After his birth, his family moved to a larger cottage. During James Cook's childhood, his father worked on many different farms. His mother took care of the children and the house. She cooked meals over a fire and did laundry by hand.

The young James Cook showed great intelligence, even at an early age. His parents sent him to a school run by a local woman who taught him how to read and write and do basic math. James did chores for his teacher such as taking horses to a trough to drink. James's father claimed much of his time: As boys, James and his brother John worked almost every day alongside their father, planting, weeding, and harvesting crops, and helping him tend his employer's animals.

By 1736, the elder James Cook had been hired to serve as foreman by a farmer named Thomas Skottowe. He would be managing Skottowe's farm. This position required more than an ability to grow crops and tend animals. It took intelligence and the ability to handle money. It was a position of responsibility.

Apparently, Thomas Skottowe was impressed by young James Cook, as well as his father. Skottowe paid the boy's tuition at a nearby private school. There, James excelled at math. In his free time, he liked to explore the local countryside with his schoolmates, looking for birds' nests, picking apples, and swimming.[1]

Out Into the World

In the eighteenth century, poor children grew up quickly. They were expected to work from the time they could walk. They left home to earn their own living when they were still teenagers.

As James Cook neared the age when he would leave home, he decided he did not want to be a farmer, even though he was strong and liked the outdoors. Perhaps eager to leave the small town in which he had grown up, he moved to a nearby town named Staithes, a port located on the North Sea. This may have been the farthest he had ever traveled. Certainly he had never seen a big city like London.

In Staithes, Cook, then probably about sixteen, found a job with a storekeeper named William Sanderson, who sold groceries. Sanderson was also a haberdasher, who sold fabric, thread, buttons, and other items needed to make clothing.

Cook worked for Sanderson for just eighteen months. During that time, perhaps he realized that, while he liked working with people, he did not want to be cooped up indoors all day.

Sanderson's shop was within sight of the sea. Cook must have spent time on the wharves. He would have seen tall sailing ships anchor to unload their cargoes. Perhaps he had heard sailors talk of voyages to India and China. He might have dreamed of life on board a ship.

To Sea

After he quit his job with Sanderson, Cook left Staithes on foot. He walked to a bigger, busier port named Whitby, a big town of ten thousand people. Its harbor was often filled with ships. Businessmen there owned close to two hundred vessels. There were five shipyards in town where carpenters built new boats.

Cook had left Sanderson on good terms. In fact, his old employer had given him a suggestion about where he might find a new job. Sanderson had given Cook the names of John and Henry Walker.

The Walkers were shipowners. Their vessels carried mostly coal. Coal was then a very important commodity. It was used as fuel in homes and factories. A thousand British ships transported coal from the north to England and Europe. Four hundred ships carried coal to London alone. The busiest ships made ten voyages a year. Their crews often experienced danger. The maps available of England's east coast were poor. Its harbors had many sunken rocks and sand bars. Severe storms were frequent. Ships were often grounded and wrecked. In those days, many seamen did not know how to swim. In fact, few people knew how to swim—it was not a popular sport or recreation like it is today.

Cook spent his youth learning the skills that would later help him become a famous explorer.

In those days, most working-class people learned a skilled trade by becoming an apprentice. This meant they signed a contract in which they agreed to work for someone already established in a trade for a specified amount of time in exchange for instruction. They received no pay.

Cook was eighteen when he bound himself as an apprentice for three years to John Walker. No one knows why he had not decided to become an apprentice earlier. He was more than six feet tall and big-boned. He would always be fit and strong.

Cook liked working for Walker from the start. The Walkers were Quakers. Like most members of this religious sect, they were quiet, tolerant people. John Walker always treated the men who worked for him fairly and with kindness. This was not true of everyone in the shipping business. Some shipowners hired cruel captains to sail their ships, men who used whips and other harsh punishments on their crews. Cook never experienced this kind of treatment, although he would later use strict discipline on his own ships.

Cook became a member of the crew of a special kind of ship called a Whitby collier, designed especially to carry coal. It was flat-bottomed, broad-beamed, and bulky. Like all ships of the day, it was powered by the wind that filled the sails that hung from its masts. Colliers never went fast. They were difficult to maneuver. Compared to fast, graceful sailing ships with their sleek lines, colliers looked ugly. But they were seaworthy and could ride out many storms. They had other advantages, too. They could be easily hauled out of the water for repair. They could also carry from four hundred to six hundred tons of cargo.

Cook got his sea legs fast. He was soon very comfortable aboard a ship and did not suffer from seasickness. Like other apprentices, he started by sweeping and mopping the decks and doing other chores. He soon learned to climb up and down the collier's rigging, to adjust sails. He quickly earned more responsibility.

The ship's master and mate found Cook to be a good sailor. Cook obeyed commands and never slacked off. He asked many questions. When they found out he was interested in learning to navigate, they taught him. Navigation was a special skill that few sailors possessed. He had to learn how to steer and recognize landmarks. He also had to learn to recognize dangers like shoals and rocks lying hidden under the surface of the water.

Going to sea for more than fifty days at a time, Cook spent two years on the three-masted 450-ton *Freelove.* The ship had a crew of nineteen, including ten apprentices. It traveled the route between Newcastle-on-Tyne, a coal-shipping port in northeast England, and London.

In 1748, John Walker had a new ship built. He named it the *Three Brothers.* When it went to sea, Cook was part of its crew. The vessel carried coal not only up the west coast of England, but also to Ireland

and Norway. It transported soldiers and horses for the British Army as well.

From the beginning of his apprenticeship, Cook lived with John Walker whenever his ship was back at Whitby. Later, the Walkers remembered that Cook was never one to spend his evenings drinking at a tavern or courting a girl. Instead, he would sit at the Walkers' kitchen table and study. He practiced using a compass and reading charts. He studied astronomy and learned to calculate latitude using a special instrument called a quadrant. He gave himself math problems to solve.[2] The Walkers showed him sail plans and plans of ships.

In 1750, Cook's apprenticeship ended. Free to sign on with any ship he liked, Cook, aged twenty-two, made one more voyage on John Walker's ship, this time as a seaman, a regular sailor. Then he signed on with another coal company. Perhaps he did so because it traded at ports on the Baltic Sea, much farther than he had ever been.

In 1752, John Walker hired Cook once again. He was given an important job, as mate on the *Friendship*. This meant he was second in command. Three years later, Walker offered Cook the ship's command. This was remarkable progress. Few twenty-seven-year-olds would have been able to handle the job. To command a ship required skill as a seaman, a navigator, and a leader of men.[3]

Cook refused the offer. Historians can only guess why. It seems unlikely he doubted his own abilities.

Some scholars think he was tired of the coal trade. Others say he had been smuggling and had realized that the time had come to get out of the business, before he was caught. Historian Hugh Cobbe suggests that he had found out other members of his crew were smugglers.[4] He might not have wanted to deal with them. Perhaps Cook was moved by love of his country. At that time, in 1755, war was looming between England and France. This would become the war known in America as the French and Indian War. In Europe, it would be called the Seven Years' War. Perhaps Cook wanted to help defend his native land. Or maybe he realized that there would soon be new opportunities for advancement in the British Navy.

The Navy and Wartime Service

For whatever reason, James Cook left John Walker to enlist in 1755 in the Royal Navy as an able seaman, a sailor who was not an officer. Walker later remembered, "he had always an ambition to go into the Navy."[5] Cook was assigned a berth on the sixty-gun ship *Eagle*. Within a month, he was promoted from able seaman to the higher position of master's mate. He then started to keep a log in which he recorded the ship's speed, mileage, and other important matters. Navy officials immediately noticed his ability. He continued to perform well. His ship first helped blockade the French coast and then sailed for Canada.

In 1757, Cook received a promotion to ship's master. This meant he was responsible, under the captain, for navigating the ship. At its helm, he charted the St. Lawrence River, which runs across Quebec, Canada, from Lake Ontario to the Gulf of St. Lawrence. This was a very important task. The St. Lawrence had been recognized as a major seaway for more than a hundred years, but it had not yet been accurately mapped because of its many tricky channels. Cook did a "meticulous" job.[6] The beautiful charts he drew were extremely detailed. They showed not just the many twists and turns of the river but also gave information about its shores. He drew in wharves and piers. But the charts' most important details were the numbers and notes Cook included about the water. They showed how deep passages were and where hidden rocks and timbers were located. Cook's charts made it possible for the British to attack the French-Canadian city of Quebec. The British staged a great assault on the city in 1759, which ultimately led to its surrender.

Cook remained in Canada until November 1762. He made many more charts for the Royal Navy, then he returned to England.

Starting a Family

Six weeks after setting foot on his native shore, James Cook got married. How he came to meet Elizabeth Batts is no longer known, but a copy of their marriage certificate still exists. Over the next seventeen years, James and Elizabeth Cook would have six children together. Three of them died as infants.

James Cook would never have a great deal of time to devote to his family. In fact, he was back at sea just four months after his wedding. Apparently, Elizabeth never complained or tried to persuade Cook to leave the Navy. For the rest of his life, he would often be gone for many months, sometimes even years, at a time.

Between 1762 and 1767, the Royal Navy sent Cook on five more voyages to Canada. He continued his survey work. In 1764, he was given command of the schooner *Grenville.* Its mission was to survey the eastern coasts of Canada. This task took four years to complete. Every winter, Cook returned home to England, where he made the information he had collected into charts. His excellent charts were still being used until the early part of the twentieth century.

Navy officials valued Cook highly because of his skills as a navigator and cartographer. They also praised him because he got along well with the men under his command. He treated them as Walker had treated him, fairly and with kindness. These traits would serve Cook well in the years ahead.

Chapter 5

Cook's First Voyage of Exploration

In the mid-1760s, the Royal Society, an organization of thinkers, scholars, and scientists, persuaded the British government to sponsor a special voyage of exploration. Naval officer James Cook would lead the expedition, which began in the summer of 1768. In doing so, he would make history.

This expedition launched what historian William H. Goetzmann called the Second Great Age of Discovery.[1] Earlier, explorers had searched mainly for new lands to conquer and riches to claim. Scientists had gone along only occasionally. Now, exploration began to have a scientific aspect. Explorers focused on mapping the earth and recording what they observed—rocks, minerals, fossils, plants, animals, and people. Returning home, explorers shared their specimens and notes, published books, and held exhibitions for the public.

Exploration such as James Cook undertook required great courage and intelligence. He headed, after all, into the great unknown. The voyage included many dangers such as storms at sea and fierce animals.

The Transit of Venus

The Royal Society wanted to sponsor Cook's first expedition because its members were obsessed with finding out exactly how far Earth is located from the Sun. They knew one way they could determine this was to time the planets' transits across the Sun. (Astronomers use the word *transit* to mean the passage of a small celestial body across the disk of a larger celestial body. Humans can see this from Earth when another planet passes in its orbit between Earth and the Sun.) This measurement would yield the data they needed to calculate Earth's distance from the Sun.[2]

Astronomers had made several attempts to measure planets' transits across the Sun between 1639 and 1761. Because of the nature of the orbits of Earth and Venus, every hundred years or so, humans can observe the transit of Venus twice in the space of just a few years. One transit had occurred in 1761. Scientists knew the next would occur in 1769.

Before either transit had occurred, a cartographer named Joseph Nicholas Delisle organized a joint observation. In 1760, he published a map showing the best places from which to observe the transit. One hundred twenty observers watched the transit from sixty different locations, including Peking, Calcutta, Constantinople, Rome, the Cape of Good Hope, Newfoundland, Siberia, Isle Rodriguez in the Indian Ocean, and St. Helena in the South Atlantic.[3] They compared notes, but varying weather conditions, different instruments, and faulty math tables meant they needed still more data.

So scientists laid plans for a second coordinated observation of the transit of Venus in 1769. The next transit would not take place for another hundred years. Astronomers once again spread out over the globe. British scientists decided that one observation needed to be made from the island of Otahiti (present-day Tahiti), which British Navy officer Samuel Wallis had just "discovered" on an expedition he undertook in 1766 and 1767.

An Expedition Is Planned

British King George III agreed to fund the expedition. He gave the Royal Society four thousand pounds, a very large sum of money at the time, to pay for equipment and pay the expenses of a scientific party. He also agreed to give the society use of a Navy ship with a crew of sailors. He did so in the name of scientific progress.

But there were also other reasons for the government to sponsor the voyage. Great Britain was seeking to build an empire. It wanted to claim more land. It

King George III sponsored Cook in his first voyage to the Pacific.

also wanted to expand its economy, so it could trade more around the world. At the same time, British officials wanted to prevent other countries from expanding their size or influence. Great Britain's main rival was France, which had already settled the Falkland Islands, located south of the equator and east of South America.[4] Great Britain feared the further expansion of France's influence in the Southern Hemisphere.

Choosing a Commander

The Royal Society had wanted Alexander Dalrymple, the geographer who had argued that Terra Australis Incognita must exist, to be the commander of the historic expedition. However, Sir Edward Hawke, the Navy official assigned to oversee the expedition's organization, would not permit it. He is said to have stated, "he would suffer his right hand to be cut off rather than sign such . . . a commission."[5] Hawke knew Dalrymple did not have the right kind of experience to command a long and dangerous sea voyage. An experienced navigator, a Navy officer, was needed.[6] Hawke said he would choose a commander and approve the commander's choice of crew members.

There were many excellent Navy officers available who ranked higher than James Cook. But Cook was the one selected for the command. By this time, he had served twelve years in the Navy. He was a married man with three children, but this would not prevent him from agreeing to make a long and dangerous voyage. His wife had known when they married that he would be away for long stretches of time. Hawke selected Cook because of his experience in navigation and cartography, in particular. Cook was also known to treat his crew fairly. Sailors performed admirably under Cook.

Cook was also known to be interested in science, especially astronomy. In 1766, he had observed an eclipse of the Sun while in Newfoundland and sent his calculations to the Royal Society. Such past efforts made him an attractive candidate to the Society. Its members judged him "a good mathematician and very expert in his business."[7] Right after his appointment was announced, in May 1768, Cook was promoted by the Navy to lieutenant.

The *Endeavour* and Its Crew

The Navy had already selected a ship for the expedition. It was named the *Endeavour*. It was a collier, just like the one Cook had sailed on while he was in the coal business. Its design made it sturdy and roomy. Cook also knew from experience that it could maneuver well along tidal coasts and sail channels whose depths had not been tested. He described the ship as "what in my opinion was most to the purpose."[8] It was a small vessel, only 106 feet long and just under 30 feet wide.

Cook ordered supplies to last him a year at sea. These included such items as beer and brandy, ballast (iron and coal to weigh the ship down and make it stable), cannons and guns, salt, life jackets made of cork, and surgeon's supplies. The list went on and on. To eat, there would be salt beef, salt pork, biscuits, raisins, sugar, oatmeal, and sauerkraut. Sauerkraut is pickled cabbage. Cook took it along because he hoped it would help prevent scurvy, an often fatal disease people develop when they do not eat enough vitamin C. Scurvy causes bleeding gums, easy bruising, and weakness.

Cook also asked for scientific instruments. He wanted surveying instruments—a theodolite, a plane table, and an azimuth compass. These were tools he would need for making accurate maps and charts. He would also use the theodolite when observing the transit of Venus. To trade with any native peoples he met, he took along nails, mirrors, fishhooks, hatchets, beads, scissors, and dolls.

Next, Cook selected his crew. This was a difficult and important job. The men chosen would have to live in a small space and work together for a very long period of time. Several of Cook's crew members had been with Samuel Wallis when he "discovered" Tahiti. Cook's officers included Zachary Hicks as second lieutenant, another lieutenant, an American named John Gore, soon-to-be third lieutenant Charles Clerke, ship's master Robert Molyneux, and master's mates Richard Pickersgill and Francis Wilkinson. The surgeon was William Brougham Monkhouse, and his assistant was William Perry. The crew of eighty-five also included a dozen marines, forty able seamen, and a handful of midshipmen.[9] Most members of the crew were Englishmen, although a few came from elsewhere in Europe. There were a Brazilian and two Americans. Following naval custom, Cook's sons, ages five and six, were recorded as going along as a servant and a carpenter, but they did not in fact go on the voyage. Cook just signed them up so that they could rise to lieutenant while they were still young men if they chose to pursue a career in the Navy.[10]

The Royal Society's Preparations

At the same time, the Royal Society selected its official Venus observers. One of these was Charles Green. The other was Cook himself.[11] Green had worked at Greenwich in the Royal Observatory. The Society also requested that Joseph Banks be allowed to go. Banks, although only twenty-five years old, was a rich man. His family had made a fortune from "scientific" farm management. Their farm was seen as a model. They had drained their land and experimented with different crops. After going to Oxford University, Banks became a naturalist, a scientist who studies nature. In 1766, he sailed on a naval vessel to Newfoundland, where he studied exotic plants and animals.[12] He may have met Cook there. Throughout his life, he would use his wealth to sponsor scientific studies and exploration. Banks provided money to pay much of the scientific expenses of the voyage.

Two artists, Alexander Buchan and Sydney Parkinson, also went along with the expedition to draw

Source Document

Rules to be observ'd by every person in or belonging to His Majesty's Bark the Endeavour....

    1st To endeavour by every fair means to cultivate a friendship with the Natives and to treat them with all imaginable humanity.

    2nd A proper person will be appointed to trade with the Natives for all manner of Provisions, Fruit, and other productions of the earth; and no other officer or Seaman ... shall Trade or offer to Trade for any sort of Provisions, Fruit, or other productions. ...

    3rd Every person employ'd a shore on any duty is strictly to attend to the same, and if by neglect he looseth any of His Arms or working tools ... the full Value thereof will be charged againest his pay. ...

    4th The same penalty will be inflicted upon every person who is found to imbezzle, trade, or offer to trade with any of the Ship's Stores of what nature so ever. ...[13]

Captain Cook laid out strict rules for the crew of his ship, especially in regard to dealings with the native peoples they might encounter.

views and specimens. In Banks's retinue were Banks's friend Daniel Carl Solander, a naturalist, a secretary, and four people who would help collect specimens from nature.[14] Two of the men employed as collectors, Thomas Richmond and George Dorlton, were black.

Cook's Instructions

On July 30, 1768, Cook received his official instructions from the British Navy. He was to sail from England south and west to Cape Horn, the southernmost point of South America. After rounding the Cape, he was to continue to Tahiti. There, he was to anchor. The crew and scientists would go ashore to set up a camp. That would be the spot from which they would observe the transit.

Cook was advised to treat any natives he encountered in a friendly manner. He was to "endeavour by all proper means to cultivate a friendship with the Natives . . . Shewing them every kind of Civility and regard."[15] Because he was to claim all land he discovered for Great Britain, it was important that he establish peaceful relations with the natives from the very beginning. In secret, he was also told, after leaving Tahiti, to sail as far south as 40 degrees latitude, or until he reached the fabled southern continent. If he did not find it, he was then to sail west. He was to continue on until he reached new land or New Zealand, which the Dutch explorer Abel Janszoon Tasman had already sighted in 1642. Great Britain had decided the time had come to claim New Zealand for itself.

Everywhere Cook went, he was ordered to bring back records and samples of soils, plants, animals, birds, fish, and minerals. He should write down everything he learned about the natives. He was also expected to chart all the land he encountered. He was "with the Consent of the Natives to take possession of Convenient Situations in the Country in the Name of the King of Great Britain; or, if you find the Country uninhabited take Possession for His Majesty by setting up Proper Marks and Inscriptions, as first discoverers and possessors."[16]

The Voyage Begins

On August 26, 1768, the *Endeavour* sailed from Plymouth, England, with Cook in command. Six days after he left, his wife, Elizabeth, gave birth to a baby boy. Unfortunately, the baby died in less than a month.

The *Endeavour* sailed south and west around South America. Along the way, Cook once ordered two disobedient men whipped: They had refused to eat fresh beef, which Cook deemed necessary for good health. The voyage was otherwise pleasant.

Everybody delighted at the sight of flying fish. They fished for shark. Cook made lunar observations. On November 13, the *Endeavour* anchored at Rio de Janeiro, on the coast of Brazil. The Spanish officials who governed the city refused to let Banks and his colleagues visit the city. They could not believe they were scientists. They thought they must be smugglers or spies. Despite these orders, Banks sneaked onto land in a small boat one night to collect plants.

Cook did manage to take on needed supplies such as animals and other fresh foods. He also made small repairs to the ship and charted the bay. He would make more maps at every landfall and as they cruised along coastlines.

In December, the *Endeavour* was at sea once more. It soon entered the Strait of Magellan. On January 11, 1769, Cook spied Tierra del Fuego. He anchored in a harbor there. Banks and his party rowed a small boat to shore to collect plant specimens. Even though it was then midsummer, according to the Southern Hemisphere's calendar, it was extremely cold there. Two of the collectors froze to death overnight.

Back on board, Cook and his crew rounded Cape Horn. Cook and Green calculated its latitude, or the distance it lay south of the equator. They made a tiny error in calculating its longitude, or the distance it lay west of the prime meridian, which passes through Greenwich, England. They placed Cape Horn forty miles too far west on their map.

Once around the Horn, Cook sailed farther south than anyone had ever gone before. He knew that the absence of currents meant there was no nearby continent. "I do not think my self at liberty to spend time in searching for what I was not sure to find," he recorded in his journal. He headed for Tahiti.[17]

Tahiti

Cook then sailed north and west. Finding Tahiti was no simple task. Wallis had recorded his observations of its location, but explorers' estimates were often inaccurate. What Cook had to do to be sure to find Tahiti was to reach its latitude a few hundred miles east of where he thought the island lay. If he sailed westward along that line of latitude, he would almost certainly find Tahiti eventually.

On April 11, the ship's lookout spotted Tahiti's mountains. When the ship entered Matavia Bay on

In Tahiti, Cook and his crew were invited to a theater of dance. He described the women as distinguished and their clothes as elegant. He said the audience enjoyed the comic antics of four male performers even more than the dancing.

April 13, 1769, Cook and the others were met by hundreds of Tahitians in canoes, carrying green leaves signaling peace and crying "Taio, taio!" which translates as *comrade*.[18] The Tahitians would continue to treat Cook and the other men with great friendliness throughout their stay.

Everyone disembarked and set up what they called Fort Venus, a camp with buildings surrounded by a wall with swivel guns, or cannons. Banks noted that what he saw was "the truest picture of an arcadia" or paradise.[19] He predicted that the British were going to rule happily there. He and his colleagues studied the botany, zoology, and geology of the island. They collected specimens, and made notes and drawings, which would be sent to the Royal Society. Banks described the people of Tahiti in great detail.

In June, Green and Cook observed the transit of Venus. In the words of historian Hugh Cobbe, "[Unfortunately] the grand world-wide operation was a failure because a penumbra, or shadow, around the planet made accurate measurement virtually impossible, though this only emerged later."[20] In addition to their scientific work, Cook and the other sailors tended to their ship, making repairs and collecting supplies. They also took time to get to know the Tahitians. Cook ordered his crew "To endeavour by every fair means to cultivate a friendship with the Natives and to treat them with all imaginable humanity."[21] Like Banks, Cook and his officers also wrote about the people in their journals.

For the most part, Cook liked and admired the people he met, although he was annoyed by their disregard of private property, especially when someone stole his stockings from right under his own pillow. The Tahitians' existence seemed peaceful. There was an abundance of food. Cook learned some of the language and was able to talk about the geography of the South Pacific with the natives. He made a chart using what he learned. It arranged the islands according to the time it took to reach them from Tahiti by outrigger canoe.[22] He had also made another more traditional and very precise map of Tahiti that recorded its topography (the features of its land, including hills and valleys), rivers, and the depth of the waters surrounding the island. He recorded on his chart place names used by the natives.[23]

Cook's crew found plenty to eat, drink, and entertain them on Tahiti. The natives showed great curiosity about these Europeans, and made great efforts to communicate with all of them. Problems arose for Cook from time to time, however, when members of his crew fell in love with local women. Some of the crew did not want to leave Tahiti.

Cook had some fears about the consequences of his voyages. These fears were well grounded. Contact with Europeans would, in the words of historian Hugh Cobbe, "debase and all but destroy" the South Pacific.[24] After Cook's voyages, as more and more Europeans came to the islands, the Polynesian people became sick with previously unknown diseases and their culture started to fall apart.

Finally, the time came for Cook's ship to depart. An islander named Tupia and his son Tapota left with Cook. Tupia acted as translator for the rest of the voyage through Polynesia. He helped the expedition a great deal.

Cook was a careful observer. He learned to speak a little of several different Polynesian languages. He also asked natives across Polynesia questions through Tupia and other interpreters. His observations led him to believe that the different native populations were related even though they were widespread. But he saw differences between their societies, too. Some were war-like people. Others were peaceful. Some islands were ruled by cruel chiefs who exerted complete control over their people. On other islands, the people had more say in government.

Cook also recorded differences in the islanders' diets. On barren atolls, they ate mostly fish. On islands with rich soil, however, natives farmed, raising animals and cultivating plants. He also discovered that not all Polynesian islands have a plentiful supply of fresh water. The matter of recording the natives' diet and water supply was not just of scientific interest to Cook. He was trying to find the best places for later British ships to stop to take on supplies while sailing the South Pacific.

Far South

Leaving Tahiti on July 13, 1769, Cook headed west. Sailing past the seventy atolls of the Society Islands, he discovered, named, and claimed them for his king.[25] On August 9, he turned south. The *Endeavour* continued until it reached the 39° of latitude. Then it sailed west.

On October 6, Cook sighted New Zealand. He and his men were the first Europeans actually to set foot on the islands. Tasman, the first European to sight New Zealand in 1642, had never landed there. No European had even approached the islands for more than one hundred years.

Banks believed that, in reaching New Zealand, Cook's expedition had found the fabled southern continent. Cook disagreed. He dropped anchor in a bay. He wanted to send men ashore to get fresh water. Then he planned to survey the coast. He landed two small boats on shore.

As he walked toward some huts, some Maori natives appeared from the woods. Those crew members left behind to guard the boats became frightened and fired at the natives, killing one. Cook and his men then boarded the boats and rowed back to the *Endeavour.* The following day, Cook returned and a translator talked with the Maori for him. Unfortunately, more fighting would break out over the next couple of days. Cook had met a people who were used to fighting all the time. The Maori were also afraid of him and the other British. In their oral history, the Maori would describe the white Europeans as goblins.

Cook was distressed at the lives his men took. However, he was also relieved that none of his men had been killed.

After the encounter with the Maori, Cook sailed farther north. There, he found friendlier people. Then he sailed around the two islands of New Zealand. To go around them took the *Endeavour* six months. It was not an easy sail. The ship encountered fierce storms. Day after day and night after night, the crew struggled with the sails and rigging, trying to keep the ship upright and on course.

Cook was an interested observer. He sketched the lands he saw and made maps and charts based on his observations. He also recorded his observations in his ship's log and his own journal. He practiced observing natural phenomena. He noticed, for example, that certain patterns in the water meant there were shoals and reefs beneath the surface. He also practiced watching the sky, learning to predict changes in the weather.

Circling New Zealand, Cook had many happy encounters with natives, unlike the violent incident with the Maori. Cook traded with several peoples. He learned that some were cannibals—he was given a half-eaten human head as a gift. This did not alarm him, however. He always displayed great courage. He was also remarkable in that he seldom judged the people he met. Unlike most Europeans of his day, he did not regard them as primitive or less sophisticated than

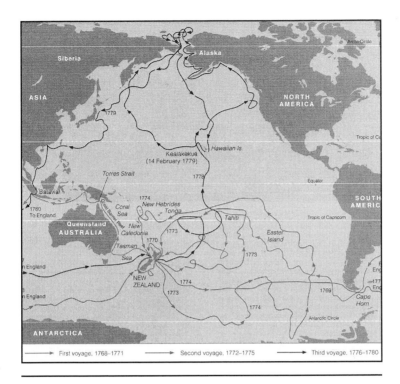

Captain Cook explored New Zealand and sailed along the coast of Australia.

the people of Europe. In his log, he noted that the Maori built excellent boats and fortified villages. Local legends continued to tell of Cook's kindness a hundred years after his voyage.

Australia

Finished surveying the islands, Cook decided to head west for home. His official instructions from the Royal Navy had been to search for a new continent south and west of Tahiti until he reached new land or New Zealand. Having reached New Zealand, he had fulfilled his mission. It was time to go back to England.

Cook thought good winds would make the trip home around Africa's Cape of Good Hope easier than another trip around South America's Cape Horn. So he headed west. On April 19, 1770, he sighted eastern Australia, which he claimed for his king.

Cook's men landed on a site inhabited by natives who he recognized were not Polynesian. He found the people impressive in terms of physique. They seemed generally to be happy people. Apparently, they had everything they wanted: They accepted but then discarded presents from Cook. He took this to mean that they wished to be friendly, but did not need the gifts he offered.

From his first landfall, he sailed north for ten days until he found safe harbor in Botany Bay. There, Banks and his fellow scientists gloried in the many new kinds of plants they found. Cook described the people they found there, saying, "In reality they are far happier than we Europeans . . . The Earth and sea of their own accord furnishes them with all things necessary for life."[26] But while Banks and Cook considered Australia a place well worth scientific investigation, they did not regard it as a paradise, as they had the South Sea islands.

As they continued up the Australian coast, they encountered the treacherous Great Barrier Reef, a long coral reef that runs along the coast of Australia. For 1,250 miles, they had to move forward at an agonizingly slow pace. Cook posted men all over the ship's rigging to try to spot dark shadows of coral. They navigated safely for one thousand miles, but then hit a pinnacle, or high point. The ship was stuck. The entire crew was in terrible danger of drowning. Sailors manned the pumps, but still, four feet of water covered the ship's bottom at high tide.

Cook remained calm as always. He ordered a sail filled with oakum (jute fiber coated with tar that was used to caulk ships), wool, rope, and dung to be slung under the ship. It was pulled tight in the hope that suction might make a plug.[27] Cook's plan worked. Water stopped pouring in.

Cook sailed on and beached the ship a few miles later, in a safe area. Cook discovered that coral had actually worked its way into the hole in the ship. The crew had to stay there for two months to repair the *Endeavour.* Finally, in August 1770, they made it through the Torres Strait between New Guinea and Australia. They made more repairs there, and then, they were able to sail for home.

Cook reached Batavia, as Djakarta, the capital of Indonesia, was then known, on October 10, 1770. From there, he sent home a copy of his journal, maps, and a report.[28] The dangerous diseases malaria and dysentery spread among the crew. The interpreters Tupia and Tapota died. English members of the crew also died at Batavia and on the way back home.

The *Endeavour* returned to England on June 12, 1771. Cook and his crew had been gone just one month less than three years.

Source Document

Saturday, 11 August 1770: . . . I came to a resolution to Visit one of the high Islands in the offing in my Boat, as they lay at least 5 Leagues out to sea and seem'd to be of such height that from the top of one of them I hoped to see and find a Passage out to sea clear of the shoals. . . .

Sunday, 12 August 1770: . . . The only Land-animals we saw here were Lizards and these seem'd to be pretty plenty which occasioned my naming the Island Lizard Island.[29]

Cook's journal from August 1770 described how he came to name one of the islands he explored briefly.

Arriving home, the *Endeavour* carried a smaller crew than it had when it first left. Almost half of the crew had died from diseases caught in Djakarta. Before that, Cook had lost only one man to disease. Those who made it home were in good spirits. They had undertaken a long and sometimes dangerous voyage in cramped quarters. They had suffered from extremes of hot and cold. At times, they had run short of food. But they had also experienced thrilling adventure and visited exotic places. They had enjoyed sailing under Cook, whom they considered fair and reasonable. They appreciated his predictable nature, because it meant they could depend on him. They also recognized him as a very hard-working man, which eased their own sense of burden.

Home Again

Back at home, Cook was happily reunited with his family. Unfortunately, he would have little time for them. He had many reports to make and meetings to attend.

One person he wrote to was his old employer, John Walker. To Walker, Cook described what he regarded as his own achievement: "I have made no very great Discoveries yet I have exploar'd more of the Great South Sea than all that have gone before me so much that little remains now to be done to have a thorough knowledge of that part of the Globe."[30] Some scientists refused to take James Cook's word that there was no southern continent. Cook himself agreed that it was "a matter . . . curious and important" and not definitively settled.[31]

At home, Joseph Banks was received as a hero. Cook received praise, too. He had won a reputation as an able and intrepid man. The Royal Navy promoted him to the rank of commander. Cook was also granted an audience with King George III, a rare honor. The monarch praised him highly.[32] But Cook's fame would continue to grow as he undertook more voyages on behalf of Great Britain.

Cook's Second Voyage, 1772-1775

After Cook returned to England from his first voyage, scientists continued to debate whether a "Great Southern Continent" existed. Cook doubted it, but he still wondered. His curiosity led him to propose making a second voyage, this time with two ships. He made his proposal in September 1771, after being home for only two months.[1]

King George III and the British Navy agreed to sponsor the trip. Cook had many aims for this voyage. He did not just want to find out more for England about the geography of the world. He wanted to make astronomical observations, and gather and catalog "nature's storehouse."[2] He was also supposed to test John Harrison's fourth chronometer, an extraordinarily accurate navigational instrument. Cook thought Joseph Banks would assist him in this since Banks had expressed his interest in going along on a second voyage. In fact, Banks would consider this *his* voyage.

The *Endeavour* needed repairs after its long voyage. It could not sail again soon. So, acting on Cook's wishes, the navy purchased two more colliers and had some changes made to them so they would be ready for a long ocean voyage. They were named the *Resolution* and *Adventure*.

One of the ships was modified especially to accommodate Joseph Banks. He had decided that the *Resolution*, the ship on which Cook intended to sail, was not big enough for him. Banks wanted to bring along a party of fifteen, including scientists, artists, secretaries, and servants. He pressured Navy officials to add a new upper deck and round house or cabin to his ship.

As the date of departure approached, Cook ordered the *Resolution* taken out on a trial run. On May 10, it sailed to the Nore, which stands in the estuary of the River Thames. Returning, the first lieutenant, Cooper, reported that the ship was top-heavy and was in danger of capsizing, or overturning.

Cook informed Banks of the bad news and ordered the new upper deck and round house cut down. His crew applauded his decision. Charles Clerke, a Navy officer who had gone on the first voyage and would be on the second voyage, wrote to Banks, "By God I'll go to Sea in a Grog Tub, if desir'd, or in the Resolution as soon as you please; but must say I think her by far the most unsafe Ship I ever saw or heard of."[3]

Banks did not take the news well. In fact, a sailor later wrote that, when Banks came to look at the ship, he "swore and stamp'd the Warfe, like a Mad Man; and instantly order'd his servants, and all his things out of the Ship."[4] He and his party would not go on the second voyage, after all. Cook wrote that Banks had made a mistake in interfering with "the choice, equipment and even Direction of the Ships[,] things that he was not a competent judge of."[5] Banks had failed to realize how much the ship *Endeavour* had had to do with his success on the first voyage. The Navy had wanted very much to please Banks, but it proved impossible to fulfill his wishes.

Personnel

Cook would have to leave without Banks. Nevertheless, the Navy easily found other scientists who were eager to go along.

This time, the scientists on board included artist William Hodges; two astronomers, William Wales and William Bayly; and John Reinhold Forster and his son George, who would study natural history.[6] Cook assembled a crew for the *Resolution* of ninety-two officers and seamen and eighteen marines. Seventy-nine men sailed on the *Adventure*. Tobias Furneaux was named commander of the *Adventure*. Many members of both crews had been on Cook's first voyage.

Laying Plans

Once again, Cook had to collect the supplies he needed for the long journey. For this voyage he would buy not just food, medicine, and other supplies, but new scientific instruments. Navigation was constantly becoming a more exact and better-equipped science. Even during the time Cook was away on his first voyage, scientists had invented better equipment. On this voyage, Wales and Bayly were to test four marine chronometers. Chronometers are extremely precise timepieces. They made precise navigation possible by determining longitude exactly. The chronometer was a huge advance in sailing technology. It changed navigation and exploration forever. For his voyage, Cook, not willing to put all his trust in the chronometer—he favored the lunar method of navigation—used the *Nautical Almanac,* which contained accurate lunar tables.[7]

One item he would not bring on this voyage was detailed instructions. This time, the Royal Navy gave Cook permission to set his own course. His instructions merely ordered him to try to confirm the existence of a great southern continent. He could go about fulfilling that requirement any way he wished.

The Voyage Begins

Cook bid his family a fond farewell. He had been home for just a little longer than one year.

The *Resolution* and the *Adventure* sailed out of Plymouth on July 13, 1772.[8] They reached the Cape of Good Hope in October. It was summer again in the Southern Hemisphere. Cook sailed due south. As he sailed, the ocean became colder and colder. Storms abounded. In December, his ships encountered treacherous ice floes—huge flat expanses of floating ice—and icebergs—big, jagged hunks of ice, of which only the tips could be seen above the water. Sometimes their size was awesome: Sailors called some "ice islands."[9] Cook wrote that on deck "[one's] arms in a very short space of time put on the appearance of icicles, and become so numbed as . . . to be totally incapable of use."[10]

Beyond the Antarctic Circle

On January 17, 1772, Cook recorded in his log an important event: The ships had crossed the Antarctic Circle, the parallel of latitude at 66° 30′ S. He knew exactly where they were because he and the astronomers had been using lunar observations and his instruments constantly to determine their latitude and longitude. He showed pride in his accomplishment, writing, "[We] are undoubtedly the first and only ship that ever crossed that line."[11]

They sailed on. On February 8, 1772, the *Adventure* got lost in a fog. Cook and Furneaux had decided earlier what to do in case this happened. They had agreed to meet in New Zealand if the ships became separated.

Cook continued sailing as far south as possible. On March 16, Cook had to admit he could go south no farther. He could see no passage in the great mass of ice ahead. Looking at his route on the map, it is easy to see how close he came to the continent of Antarctica. But he was never to know about that

Source Document

Whether the unexplored part of the Southern Hemisphere be only an immense mass of water, or contain another continent, as speculative geography seemed to suggest, was a question which had long engaged the attention, not only of learned men, but most of the maritime powers of Europe. To put an end to all diversity of opinion about a matter so curious and important, was his Majesty's principal motive in directing this voyage to be undertaken, the history of which is now submitted to the public. . . .[12]

Captain Cook, in his record of the 1772 voyage, outlined King George's reasons for sponsoring the trip.

continent. Had he discovered it, he would have satisfied scientists' curiosity about the great southern land. However, it would have been of little benefit to Great Britain. The frozen land was not suitable for colonization and yielded no riches.

New Zealand

After heading back north, Cook sailed east for New Zealand, where he dropped anchor. His men must have cheered at the sight of land and the thought of fresh water: They had traveled ten thousand, nine hundred miles without seeing land.[13]

After spending six weeks resting and repairing their ship, Cook and his men hoisted anchor and sailed north to Queen Charlotte Sound. There, with great joy, they were reunited with the *Adventure.* By now, it was winter, which meant they could not sail south. So Cook issued orders to sail for Tahiti.

Cook was glad to go back to Tahiti. His crew stayed there two weeks. Two natives, named Odiddy

Source Document

Monday 6th September 1773
In the morning I sent the tradeing party a shore as usual and after breakfast went my self when I found that one of the natives had been a little troublesome, this fellow being pointed out to me completely equipped in the War habit with a club in each hand, as he seem'd to be intent on Mischief I took from him the two clubs and broke them and with some difficulty forced him to retire from the place. . . .[14]

Cook recorded in great detail the events of his voyages. This excerpt from his journals discusses his dealings with a native man in September 1773.

(sometimes his name is written as Hiti-Hiti) and Omai, agreed to go along with Cook for the rest of the voyage.[15] Odiddy was from Bora Bora, one of the Society Islands. Omai was from Raiatea, in the same group.[16]

They sailed off to search for the islands Dutch explorer Abel Tasman had sighted on his voyage in 1643. Cook found the island Tasman had called Middleburg. It was one of the Tongan Islands, which Cook called the Friendly Islands. His choice of name reflected the nature of the islands' people. In October, Cook headed back to New Zealand, from which he intended to sail south. Along the way, the *Adventure* was lost again.

Cook and the *Adventure*'s commander, Tobias Furneaux, had again picked a meeting point in case this happened. But the *Adventure* was late reaching the assigned place: Queen Charlotte Sound in New Zealand. When Furneaux arrived, Cook had already been there and departed, leaving behind a message in a bottle. Ten of the *Adventure*'s crew went ashore to try to find vegetables. They were captured and eaten by native Maori people. Furneaux decided he had had enough of this dangerous voyage. He headed for England, arriving home an entire year before Cook.

South Once More

In the meantime, Cook, having decided he could not wait to find the *Adventure,* headed south again. His crew fought the ice for hundreds of miles. Twice, his ship crossed the Antarctic Circle. On January 30,

1774, the ship reached 71° 10′ S latitude. The men were just 1,250 miles from the South Pole, the southernmost point on Earth. Cook could have gone still farther south, but he realized it was a "dangerous and rash enterprise and what I believe no man in my situation would have thought of."[17] George Vancouver, a midshipman of age sixteen, climbed out onto the bowsprit when he heard the ship was about to turn around. The future explorer wanted to be the person who reached the farthest point south.

Cook had mixed feelings about giving up his quest for the fabled southern continent. He knew his crew was tired and that the men would enjoy returning to a warmer part of the world. He wrote in his journal, "I whose ambition leads me not only further than any other man has been before me, but as far as I think it possible for man to go, was not sorry at meeting with this interruption [the ice]. . . ."[18] But he did have regrets: He would have liked to find out once and for all whether a southern continent existed. However, he realized that, if it did, it was so far south as to be probably uninhabitable. He thought he had done all that was humanly possible.

Cook then decided to see more of the South Seas and its islands. Over the next six months, he visited Easter Island (home to strange statues that made him "[wonder] how they were set up, indeed if the Island was once Inhabited by a race of Giants 12 feet high"), the Marquesas, Tahiti (where Odiddy left the expedition), Espiritu Santa, the New Hebrides, and New Caledonia.[19]

Everywhere, Cook described the peoples and the sights in his log. He collected artifacts such as carvings, baskets, and other items decorated with shells and beads. The artists who accompanied him sketched and painted everything they saw. William Hodges's views of Tahiti included detailed drawings of amazing outrigger canoes.[20]

Cook and his men made a final stop in New Zealand in October. Then they headed for home.

Source Document

The Inhabitants of this isle from what we have been able to see of them do not exceed six or seven hundred souls and a bove two thirds of these are Men, they either have but a few Women among them or else many were not suffer'd to make their Appearance. . . . They are certainly of the same race of People as the New Zealanders and the other islanders, the affinity of the Language, Colour and some of their customs all tend to prove it.[21]

Cook took great pains to describe the peoples he met in great detail.

They celebrated Christmas off Tierra del Fuego. On December 28, 1774, they reached the Atlantic Ocean. They arrived home on July 29, 1775.

This time, almost all of Cook's crew had survived the dangerous and exciting voyage. Cook had experimented with diet, making sure the crew had plenty of fresh produce to eat. Thus they had not suffered from scurvy. He had also paid close attention to cleanliness. This had an almost miraculous effect: Out of a crew of 118, only one man was lost to disease.

The lords of the admiralty, the highest-ranking Navy officials, talked to Cook at great length the very day he arrived home. They expressed great interest in his stories and astonishment at all he had accomplished. Cook then went off to see his wife.[22] He had been gone for three years. His family celebrated his arrival. His son James was then twelve. He was already enrolled at the Naval Academy. Nathaniel was eleven. A third son, Hugh, would be born in May 1776.

But Cook did not spend all his time catching up with his family. He sat right down at his desk to write to friends, colleagues, and well-wishers. He sent friendly messages to his old employer, John Walker, and to Joseph Banks, who was then away from London. Apparently, there was no ill feeling between Cook and Banks. Banks would soon begin going through the amazing specimens Cook had brought back.

Cook filed a final report on his voyage. Then the navy promoted him to post-captain. He was offered retirement but refused. Instead, he accepted a new post at the Navy's Greenwich Hospital.

What Had Cook Achieved?

Many historians consider this period the pinnacle of Cook's career. He was at the peak of his physical and mental powers. He was a great commander who inspired Navy crews to perform at their best. He was an able sailor, too, who excelled at keeping his ships in great shape. He would be described as a model of perseverance, dedication, and seamanship.[23]

During his second voyage, Cook had traveled seventy thousand miles. He had circumnavigated the globe at 60° S latitude. He had come very close to Antarctica. His other captain, Furneaux, had been the first ever to circumnavigate the world west to east. By traversing large areas of the South Pacific, Cook had shown the world that a southern continent, if it did indeed exist, would be a frigid wasteland and not an economically valuable addition to the British Empire. He wrote, "The Southern Hemisphere [has been] sufficiently explored and a final end put to the searching after a Southern Continent." He went on to say, "that there may be a Continent or large tract of land near the Pole. . . ."[24] Cook's reports showed a southern continent might still exist, but they dispelled the myth that it would be rich and lovely.

Cook was awarded recognition as a hero. He had a second audience with the king, who showered him with praise. The Royal Society also lauded him. They elected him a member in this very elite group. In the spring of 1776, Cook would contribute a paper on the health of seamen to the Society's journal.[25] For this report, he received the Royal Society's Copley Gold Medal.

The Navy was especially pleased with Cook's maps and charts. He had charted many of the South Pacific islands in incredible detail, and carefully calculated their locations. Modern geographers show that his calculations were correct. He had begun to get a good idea of just how many South Sea islands existed and how sophisticated their cultures were.

Public interest in Cook's discoveries ran high. The artists who had accompanied him had made sketches and paintings while on the voyage. They made more paintings from their drawings after they arrived home. Many of their works went on exhibit. Engravings from the expedition were widely published. The interpreter Omai had come to England with Cook and his crew. He was introduced to British society. Many curious people wanted to meet him.

Cook's Journals

His new position at the hospital required virtually nothing of Cook. In his free time, he worked on writing an official account of his explorations. Since he had first joined the Navy, he had kept journals, recording on a day-to-day basis what occurred while he was on board ship. He always noted technical details such as winds, his course, and the distance he sailed. He also devoted space to "Remarkable Occurrences."

John Reinhold Forster had wanted to write the official history of Cook's second voyage. But when he gave a writing sample to the Navy's Lord Sandwich, Sandwich realized it was not good enough. Sandwich knew Cook had kept a journal during the trip. He proposed that Forster and Cook write the history together.

Cook worked hard to improve his writing style. He tried hard to write clearly. It would eventually become clear, however, that Forster was never going to finish his part of the book. Cook's account alone appeared as two volumes in May 1777. They included seven hundred pages plus appendices. There were also sixty-three engravings, including twelve maps.

A New Voyage

James Cook may have been busy in London, but he still yearned to return to the sea. He would receive one last opportunity to do so.

From the time Cook's ship, the *Resolution,* docked, the Navy had assumed that it would one day begin a new voyage, to take Omai home. The *Resolution* had arrived home in fine shape and had been refitted. The *Adventure,* commanded by Furneaux, on the other hand, had arrived in bad shape. It could not go to sea again. Cook helped the Navy find a replacement for it: another collier, the *Diligence* (later renamed *Discovery*).

John Montagu, the earl of Sandwich and first lord of the admiralty, held a dinner party. Cook was among the guests with whom Sandwich discussed the issue of who should lead a third Pacific expedition to take Omai home. The expedition would do more than return Omai: "It was to be a voyage of large scope and possibly immense consequences."[26]

Lord Sandwich did not ask Cook outright to lead it. Rather, Cook volunteered. Sandwich then raced to the king with the great news.

On February 10, 1776, Cook wrote a letter and formally applied for the job. The Navy replied, giving him the mission the very same day. Cook then got to work preparing. The purpose of this third voyage was to search for the Pacific end of the fabled Northwest Passage.

Cook's Third Voyage, 1776-1779

For centuries, people believed there had to be a water passage across North America from the Atlantic to the Pacific Ocean. Explorers including Martin Frobisher, John Davis, William Baffin, and William Hudson had already searched for it, but no one had found it. Greek Captain Juan de Fuca had searched the Pacific coast in vain for its outlet. Many countries hoped to find what people thought would be a short and easy route to China.

Great Britain's Interest in the Northwest Passage

The king of England, George III, wanted to find the Northwest Passage in order to increase Great Britain's trade with China and other countries in the Orient. He also realized that it would soon be necessary to protect

Great Britain's whaling interests, as more ships of other nations began to hunt whales off the Atlantic coast of North America. He agreed to send a Navy vessel to Baffin Bay, which separates Greenland from Canada's Baffin Island, to search for the eastern end of the Northwest Passage. Now the decision was made to send Cook to the Pacific to find the Northwest Passage's western outlet. The British Navy hoped he could then sail inland, tracing it. The ship from Baffin Bay was supposed to sail west at the same time. The hope was that the explorers would meet somewhere in the middle of the North American continent.

Cook clearly preferred activity to quiet, so he volunteered to take part in this new exploration. There were advantages to his going. He was promised a reward of £20,000 (British money) if he found the Northwest Passage. The king may also have promised to promote him to the rank of admiral in the Navy.

Preparations

Cook wanted to sail at the end of April 1776, but he was not ready by then. Again, it took a long time to assemble a crew and supplies. This time, he did not pay close attention to the refitting of his ship, the *Resolution*. Later on, he would regret this decision when he discovered at sea that the Navy Yard had done a poor job of making repairs.

Cook had decided the *Adventure* would not be his second ship, but the tiny vessel named *Discovery*. Charles Clerke was supposed to command it, but at the last minute he could not go along. He was sent to prison for a time because he had guaranteed debts for his brother, who had failed to pay. He would join the expedition late.

Omai, who would be returned home during the voyage, came with a great amount of cargo. He had received many gifts from the English, including wine, gunpowder, muskets, armor, a hand organ, tin soldiers, and a globe. Cook expected that once Omai got home he would want to return to England. He did not intend to allow this. He thought Omai belonged in the South Pacific.

The Speaker of the House of Commons, Sir Fletcher Norton, threw a going-away dinner for Cook and his officers in June 1776. On June 24, Cook said good-bye to his family, picked up Omai, and left London for Plymouth, where he would board his ship.[1] The Navy had agreed to make Elizabeth Cook, the commander's wife, an allowance Cook described as very liberal.[2]

The Voyage Begins

The *Resolution* sailed on July 12, 1776. The ship immediately began to leak. Cook stopped at Tenerife, in the Canary Islands, to make repairs. Departing after a few weeks, he sailed west until he encountered a trade wind that carried the *Resolution* down along the coast of Brazil. On October 17, the ship's lookout sighted Cape Horn. Cook stopped in Cape Town. The *Discovery* caught up with the *Resolution* there on

November 10. The ships were caulked (had their seams filled) and the crew bought more supplies.

Cook left Cape Horn determined to see if he could find some islands a French captain had told him lay between lines of latitude 46° and 47°. Horrible storms made the going difficult, but he did eventually find what he named the Prince Edward Islands (present-day Narion and the Crozet islands).

The sheep and goats Cook carried for food died from the cold as his ship headed south. Fog hit during December. The *Resolution* and *Discovery* had to keep in contact by firing their guns.

On December 24, Cook found Kerguelen, also named Christmas, Island. There, he and his men celebrated Christmas in what he would name Christmas Harbour. On shore, he found a bottle containing a record of French visits in 1772 and 1773. Cook left his own inscription on the same piece of parchment. He claimed the land for Great Britain despite the fact it was so barren he called it the Isle of Desolation.[3]

New Zealand

Before departing, Cook and Clerke agreed that, if the ships were separated, they would meet in Tasmania. Then they sailed. En route Cook lost two masts in a storm, but the ships managed to stay together. Cook saw Tasmania on January 24, 1777. On January 26, the *Resolution* and the *Discovery* anchored in New Zealand's Queen Charlotte Bay to collect wood, grass, and water.[4]

There, Cook decided not to take revenge on the natives for the "Grass Cove" incident, in which members of Furneaux's crew had been killed and eaten by Maori. The natives had feared Cook would wage war against them upon his return. He found out through a translator, however, that a fight had broken out between Furneaux's men and the natives over food. The Maori had not staged a premeditated attack on the British sailors. Cook decided that if he and his men acted carefully, they would not be in danger.

Tahiti

Cook left New Zealand on February 27. On March 29, Cook sighted Tonga.[5] He still loved what he called the Friendly Islands. He stayed there more than two months. Then he set course for Tahiti on July 17, 1777. The voyage took four weeks.

On arriving and talking to the natives, he found out that two ships, which he concluded must have been Spanish, had recently been there.[6] The islands also had a new native ruler. Cook gave presents, including a fine suit, to the new king.

While there, Omai quickly lost the respect of his fellow natives. Once on shore, he would not share his possessions. Cook decided he would bring Omai to another island to settle. Before he left, the other natives relented somewhat toward Omai and gave him a fine canoe.

In September, Cook left Tahiti. He sailed for Moorea, a high island that was visible to the north and

This king of Tonga wears a cap covered with red feathers. Cook tried in vain to buy such a cap to give to his friends in Tahiti, but could not get one at any price.

west of Tahiti. He thought there were no harbors there, but Omai led them in a canoe and showed Cook a fine harbor on the north side. The men landed. On shore, they collected hogs, breadfruit, coconuts, and hibiscus. The natives there feared Cook had come to fight. But he created peace and goodwill by giving out presents and being friendly.

On October 6, however, the situation changed. The sailors had taken some of their livestock to graze on land. One of the sailors who was supposed to watch them took something from a native without asking. The native, seeking revenge, stole a goat and gave it to the island's ruler, Mahine. Cook complained to Mahine. The first goat was returned, but then a second goat was stolen. Cook became enraged. He gathered a party of men and marched across the island, burning houses and canoes.[7] The goat was returned. His men wondered whether he had done the right thing, punishing many people for the crimes of a few.[8] Cook wrote in his journal, "I could not retreat with any tolerable credet [sic], and without giving encouragement to the people of the other islands we had yet to visit to rob us with impunity."[9]

Cook then sailed to Bora Bora, where he dropped off Omai after bargaining with the island's ruler to give Omai some land. The crew stayed to build Omai a house. On November 2, Cook again boarded his ship to depart. Omai stayed on board, saying good-bye to his British friends, until they were almost out of sight of Bora Bora. When he reached Cook, "his utmost efforts to conceal his tears failed. . . ."[10] One of the *Resolution*'s small boats carried him back to shore. "Mr. King, who went in the boat, told me that [Omai] wept all the time in going ashore," Cook wrote.[11]

Cook wanted to go to Raiatea one last time. When the ships anchored there, two crew members deserted, because they wanted to stay and live there. Cook sent sailors to find them but they could not be found. Cook concluded that natives were hiding the deserters, so he took hostages to get them to reveal the sailors' where-abouts. The natives tried to take their own hostages, in retaliation, but failed. Raiatea's chief then seized the deserters. They were brought back to Cook. The captain lashed one and put them both in irons. The native hostages were then released.

All was then ready for departure, as soon as the winds permitted. Cook wanted to head for what he called New Albion, the Pacific Coast of North America. He thought only empty ocean lay ahead and that it would take six months to cross.

On January 18, 1778, however, a lookout spied what we now call the Hawaiian Islands. Cook named them the Sandwich Islands in honor of Lord Sandwich, who had helped Cook with his career. His ships first anchored off Kauai. When Cook led his men ashore, the natives gathered on the beach and fell prostrate. They considered him a person of great power. Cook was amazed to discover they were Polynesians—he did not think they had settled so far north.[12] Cook wrote, "the very great surprise they shewed at the sight of the ships and their total ignorance of fire arms seemed to prove [ours was the first European visit]."[13]

Cook stayed in Hawaii for two weeks, going ashore three times. He considered Hawaii his most important discovery. He regretted having to leave, but he had to fulfill his responsibilities—to reach the west coast of

Captain King described this scene as a meeting between Cook and a group of priests from the island of Hawaii. Cook and other officers sit in front of a sacred building, near a huge wooden idol. They are being offered a roast pig.

North America in time to search for the Northwest Passage.

The Pacific Northwest

Leaving Hawaii, Cook sailed east for seven weeks until he reached North America. He first sighted Oregon after five weeks at sea but could find nowhere to anchor.[14]

Cook and his crew met this Nootka man on Vancouver Island during his third voyage. Cook would describe the Nootka people as friendly.

He landed on March 29, 1778, in Nootka Sound, on the west coast of Vancouver Island, off what is today Canada's British Columbia. There, he built a camp. His crew chopped down trees to make repairs to the ships' masts. The work took a month.

While in the area, they met the American Indian Nootka people. The word *Nootka* means "Go round."[15] These people lived all year along the coast in large villages. Villages joined together to form confederacies, or alliances.

The Nootka fished for food and their chiefs hunted whale in dugout canoes. Canoes were also used in warfare. These natives traded eagerly with Cook. They

Source Document

A great many canoes filled with the Natives were about the ships all day, and a trade commenced betwixt us and them, which was carried on with the Strictest honisty on boath sides. Their articles were the Skins of various animals, such as Bears, Wolves, Foxes, Dear, Rackoons, Polecats, Martins and in particular the Sea Beaver, the same as is found on the coast of Kamtchatka.[16]

Cook recorded the details of a trading session on March 30, 1778.

exchanged food, water, wood, artifacts, and pelts for metal objects.

From Vancouver Island, Cook sailed north, searching for the Northwest Passage. His lookouts kept their spyglasses trained on the coast, looking for a wide river. He found a safe place to anchor in Prince William Sound and stopped there just long enough to stop a leak in his ship.[17] On and on, the *Resolution* and *Discovery* sailed. The crew investigated every sizable river. When the winds permitted a small boat to be rowed from ship to shore, Cook sent small parties of men to follow the rivers' courses. But always, his men returned to report that they did not seem to be navigable very far.

On June 14, he spied Inuit for the first time. They were paddling a kayak in the water nearby but would not approach Cook's ships.[18] On June 19, the *Discovery* met more kayaks. Their pilots brought a message in Russian.[19] Cook realized they had had earlier contact with Europeans.

In nasty weather, the ship crossed the Bering Sea and sailed through the Bering Strait into the Arctic Ocean. It was already August. The men enjoyed hunting walrus on the ice.

Cook had hoped to explore the Arctic Ocean during the summer season. But ice blocked his way. At night, in their bunks, the sailors listened to the surging and grinding of ice. Finally, Cook sailed south, to what he realized must be the east coast of Asia. By September 6, he was back in sight of the American coast and headed south. He planned to return north the next summer. He wanted first to explore the Russian coast at Kamchatka and then go back through the Bering Strait into the Arctic once more, still searching for the Northwest Passage.[20]

Return to Hawaii

Cook sailed back to Hawaii from the island of Unalaschka in October 1778. Before he left, he gave a long letter to the master of a Russian sloop, intended for the British Navy.

Some historians believe Cook arrived back in Hawaii in a time of festival, called Makahiki. Makahiki lasts four months. At one point during this

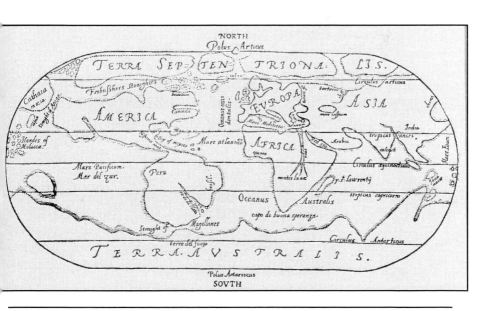

Captain Cook sailed the North Pacific, searching for the legendary Northwest Passage.

festival, a deposed god named Lono is said to reappear. The appearances of the Pleiades (a certain cluster of stars) signals his arrival.[21] Afterward, twenty-three days of feasting, games, and amusements follow.

According to historian Marshall Sahlins, Cook arrived just days after this festival began. He spent seven weeks cruising off the Islands. On this visit, he wanted to limit trading and contact between sailors and local women (he hoped to prevent the spread of venereal disease). As a result, his crew became disgruntled. Finally, Cook agreed to anchor. He went ashore on January 17 at Kealakekua Bay. The natives staged a ceremony in a temple at which he was "acknowledged as an incarnation of Lono [a god]."[22] Cook was given a cloak and a staff.

He rested and prepared to make another voyage to the Pacific Northwest the next summer. His time passed enjoyably. He announced in late January that his ships would soon depart. Boxing matches began among the natives two days before the crew left. The British assumed that these entertainments were being held in their honor. Boxing matches, however, marked the departure of the god Lono every year.[23]

On February 4, the British and the Hawaiians parted on good terms. Before he left, Cook told the Hawaiians sadly that he thought he might never see them again. Then he and his crew went to sea.

Four days later, a fierce storm came up. It damaged the foremast of the *Resolution* so badly that Cook was forced to return to Kealakekua Bay for repairs.

When Cook arrived off the island of Hawaii in 1779, the king and other chiefs were rowed out in huge canoes to meet him. They wore magnificent feathered cloaks and helmets.

Hundreds of natives turned out to greet the captain again. Members of Cook's crew later disagreed about the reaction of the Hawaiians to their return. A sailor named David Samwell wrote about "the abundant good nature which had always characterized [them]." He said it still could be seen on "every countenance [face]".[24] Sailor John Ledyard, on the other hand, remembered "that our former friendship was at an end."[25] According to him, relations became tense between the natives and Europeans. Perhaps the Hawaiians suspected the British had returned to settle. Although they seemed to enjoy European visits, they did not want the Europeans to stay permanently.

Death of the Captain

According to Cook's journal, the natives were becoming disrespectful and insolent. They interfered with his sailors' work, throwing stones at them. On February 13, Cook decided he would have to use force if the situation got worse.

On February 14, a native stole a small boat that had been tied to the *Discovery*. Cook wanted it back at almost any cost. He ordered his men to blockade the bay, so the natives could not leave to go fishing. He went ashore and took a chief hostage. He said the chief would be freed when the boat was returned. The chief went willingly with Cook, but on the way to the ship, other natives stepped up, protesting the chief's being taken away. Cook decided to release the chief, perhaps because he did not want a fight to break out. Then he headed toward the beach. He intended to get in a small boat and row back to his ship.

Suddenly, the natives began to shout. News had just arrived that the sailors Cook had sent to blockade the bay had killed another important chief. Angry, a Hawaiian ran up to Cook and threatened him with a dagger. Other natives brandished knives and threw stones. Cook fired his gun, killing one native man. The sailors who had come with him fired, too. They stopped only when they had to reload their guns.

Then Cook ordered his men back to the boats. As he left, he turned his back to the shore. Suddenly, he was hit from behind. A native had stabbed him in the back. He fell facedown in the water, dead. Four other sailors died along with him. The others made it to the boats and rowed out to their ships.

Charles Clerke was left in command of the expedition. He sent James King and a party in a boat toward shore to insist that the natives return Cook's body. They were kept waiting an hour, but the Hawaiians finally agreed. One member of the group, Heinrich Zimmermann, translated the natives' statement: "The god Cook is not dead but sleeps in the woods and will come tomorrow."[26] Later, the British would discover that the natives had dismembered Cook's body. Only parts of his body were returned the following day. Some historians believe he had been deified, or treated like a god. Others think he was treated like a victim of human sacrifice.[27]

One historian believed Cook was killed because he acted "rashly": "he seemed to have lost his customary understanding and sensitivity to the moods and attitudes of the local people."[28] He was feeling stressed and exasperated. He underestimated the Hawaiian people's loyalty to their chief and the courage they would summon even in the face of firearms. The natives, too, were exasperated, with

An artist's depiction of the death of Captain Cook in a violent encounter with native Hawaiians.

these European visitors who always seemed to need more and more food.

Clerke carried on with the voyage, continuing repairs. His men buried at sea those parts of Cook's body they were given. Relations with the natives were healed somewhat before the ships departed on February 22.

A Second Search for the Northwest Passage

The expedition continued without Cook. His ships went back to search for the Northwest Passage as Cook had originally planned. Clerke led the crew to

This engraving shows (in front) the winter home of the Kamchatka natives. James King described the hole in the center as "chimney, window, and entrance." In back are the summer houses, which are raised off the ground by posts and have grass walls.

Kamchatka, in Russia, on the continent of Asia, and through the Bering Strait into the Arctic Ocean. There, ice blocked their path again. They had not found the Northwest Passage. The passage, which exists, but is covered by ice, would not be found and traveled until the early twentieth century.

They returned to Kamchatka, where Clerke died of tuberculosis, a disease of the lungs.[29] John Gore took his place as commander of the expedition. Gore and James King sailed the ships home through the Indian Ocean.

When they returned to England, the crew reported on the abundance of furs they had found in the Pacific Northwest. The British realized that these furs could be traded in China for goods such as spices and silk that were in great demand in England. Cook's expedition had failed to destroy the myth of the Northwest Passage, and it had also created a new myth, of fabulous riches to be found in furs.[30] The men also brought back knowledge that Russia was expanding into North America. The British did not want the Russians to take over there and cut them out of the fur trade.

Soon, new British expeditions would be launched to the North Pacific. Historian David Mackay wrote, "The lure of a quick route to the East and a quick passage to fortune [furs] provided their own fascination, and, for Britons, gave the north Pacific an inflated importance for a short period after 1780."[31] The French would send Jean François de Galaupe de La Pérouse to the Pacific Northwest. The British sent George Vancouver on an expedition that would last from 1791 to 1795.

Mourning for Captain Cook

Word of the death of Captain Cook came to England in January 1780. His crew had sent a message home to Navy officials. Newspapers quickly spread the word. The reaction was profound. Cook was mourned deeply. The king of England was reported to have wept at the news.

Cook's family mourned, too. Elizabeth Cook was left a widow at the age of thirty-eight. Three of the six children she had had with Cook still survived (the three who had died had all passed away while their father was at sea). Within the year, however, their middle son, Nathaniel, died when the Navy ship on which he was stationed sank in a hurricane off Jamaica. The Navy had been sending Elizabeth Cook her husband's salary while he was away at sea. Now it awarded her a pension. She would also receive some of the profits when the official account of the third voyage was published.[32] Thus, Elizabeth Cook would be able to live comfortably for the rest of her life. On December 21, 1793, Hugh Cook, their youngest son, died of illness at age seventeen. He had been planning to become a minister. Just thirty-four days later, James, their oldest son, died at sea at age thirty. Elizabeth Cook herself would live to the ripe old age of ninety-three, dying in 1835.[33]

The British Navy mourned the loss of Cook but considered the expedition a great success. The voyage was again well publicized. The British public in general and scientists in particular continued to express great interest in what he had learned about Polynesia.

Chapter 8

Cook's Impact

A total of sixteen voyages, from Magellan's journey to Cook's third voyage, introduced the Pacific Ocean, including its lands and people, to Europe. Knowledge came slowly. It took European explorers more than three hundred years to "discover" all of Polynesia. In 1839, American explorer Charles Wilkes surveyed the South Pacific. While on an expedition to Antarctica, he and his men compiled accurate charts showing the area's many islands.[1]

The impact of the discovery of Polynesia on Europe was enormous. But the impact upon Polynesia was even bigger.

The Spread of Cook's Knowledge

According to historian Helen Wallis, "Europeans of the 1770s were aware that they were spectators of a great historical event, the unveiling of a new world."[2] The public clamored for news of James Cook and his finds. Scientists also expressed great interest in what Cook had learned. Natural philosophers praised Cook because he gave them new opportunities to study human nature. He began the science of "Pacific ethnography."[3] Ethnographers work to describe specific human cultures. After Cook's voyages, ethnographers began to study the various Pacific cultures.

In part to help satisfy the public's curiosity, Cook's voyages were well publicized. James Cook had written his own account of his second voyage. His journal and logs were used to create an official account of the third voyage. When this account was published in 1784, it sold out in just three days.[4] The British Navy immediately authorized a second edition. Many members of Cook's expeditions wrote accounts of their experiences and had them published, too.

The artists who had accompanied Cook also displayed the many pictures they had made. Many of the originals were copied by engravers whose works appeared in books or were sold as prints. Most of these artworks idealized Polynesia.

The scientists also came home from the voyages with plant and animal specimens that the thinkers of the day were eager to see. The British Museum opened a special South Seas room to which enthusiastic crowds flocked.

The European View of the South Seas

Many British people formed a view of South Pacific islanders as savages. Historian Peter Bellwood believed James Cook himself did not hold this view. He wrote, "James Cook himself was clearer-headed than this [. . .] his journals, together with those of his colleague Joseph Banks, are perhaps the most important ever written on Polynesian societies."[5] He refused to treat the Polynesians as less sophisticated than other people.

Public interest in Omai, the native man who had traveled to Europe, continued even after he returned home to the South Pacific. He became the subject of a play, *Omai: or a Trip round the World.* It was staged in 1785. In Paris, France, a ballet was performed titled *La Mort du Captaine Cooke,* or "The Death of Captain Cook," in 1789.[6]

Cook's discoveries greatly added to the British Empire at a time when Great Britain also lost a huge territory—the American colonies.[7] While Cook was making his voyages, the colonies had won their independence in what is known in the United States as the American Revolution. The places Cook claimed for his king became British colonies. This did not happen immediately, however. It took time for the British to launch new colonizing expeditions. Meanwhile, other European countries, too, would colonize Pacific islands not claimed by Great Britain. Thus Cook's voyages made an impact on Europe by expanding its empires to an entirely new part of the world.

Impact on the South Seas

In the years after Cook's death, many other Europeans explored the South Pacific. European ships again anchored at Hawaii seven years after Cook's death. British Navy Captain John Meares recorded that, when his ship anchored, many Hawaiians came in canoes to meet him. Many begged to be taken to Great Britain and talked of their "beloved Cook."[8]

Then fur traders from European countries went to Hawaii, on their way to the Pacific Northwest. British trader James Colnett visited in 1788 and 1791. British

Cook anchored in this harbor off the island of Huahine, in what is now French Polynesia, in October 1777. His two ships appear in this engraving, on the right.

explorer George Vancouver, who had started his career in the British Navy under Cook, stopped there in 1794. George Little, an American sailor, wrote that in 1809 he had visited the beautiful spot where Hawaiians told him they had buried Cook's bones.[9]

Cook made a permanent impact on the nature of exploration. Later explorers learned from Cook's experience. Like him, they set multiple goals for their expeditions. They sought not just to locate or map new lands, but also to record their impressions of what they found there. When the French sent out an expedition to the South Pacific, they named their ships *Le Geographe* and *Le Naturaliste,* indicating that knowledge of geography and nature were their goals, rather than conquest.

Across Polynesia, the fortunes of the natives declined rapidly. Cook's voyages had two terrible unintentional results. First, his crew and later voyages introduced European diseases to Polynesia, to which the natives had no immunity. Many native people died as victims of these previously unknown diseases. Second, Polynesians were exposed to firearms for the first time when they saw Cook and his crew carrying them. Later, European explorers traded guns to Polynesians. According to historian Peter Bellwood, guns led to an increase in local warfare, especially in New Zealand.[10] These wars led to shifts in power. New royal dynasties emerged in the Tongan, Hawaiian, and Society Islands, but they could not hold back forever the "tide of change" caused by encounters with

Europeans.[11] Gradually, Polynesian culture crumbled, as Polynesians began to imitate the Europeans' lifestyle. Native governments were replaced by administrations put in place by the European countries that colonized the various islands.

Missionaries—men and women sent by religious organizations in Europe to convert natives to Christianity—also had an impact. They arrived with good intentions, but they saw natives not as noble, but as "benighted [morally in the dark]."[12] They saw themselves as doing a good thing in dismantling native culture, in making Polynesians ashamed of their beliefs. According to historian Helen Wallis, "the well-intentioned work of the missionaries removed the lynchpin of social activity, religion and its attendant ritual, leaving no comparable focus in its place."[13] Polynesians lost much of their self-respect. The missionaries did benefit the natives in one way, however. They insisted that the Polynesians be allowed to continue to own their own land rather than be forced to pass into the hands of companies owned by Europeans.[14]

In 1874, one observer predicted that Europe would soon own and control all of Polynesia. This prophecy did not completely come true. Polynesian populations did decrease, but the native peoples were not wiped out entirely. In the twentieth century, the populations began to increase once more. As time went by, natives expressed renewed interest in their ancestors' traditions. Archaeologists and anthropologists launched

A young woman of the Sandwich (now Hawaiian) Islands

new studies of Polynesian cultures, which also increased respect for them.

Hawaii, the Society Islands, and New Zealand— the most important of the Polynesian cultures Cook encountered—all changed greatly after his voyages.

In Hawaii, the Islands came for the first time under a single ruler, King Kamehameha, in 1810. During the reign of his grandson, Kamehameha III, Europeans became advisors to the throne, but Hawaii remained independent. After 1876, Americans began to have an especially large influence there. The United States and Hawaii signed a trade treaty that greatly increased the amount of sugar grown in Hawaii for shipment to the United States. Americans invested heavily in Hawaiian sugar plantations. In the late nineteenth century, Americans took away some of the Hawaiian monarch's power when they forced him to modify the country's constitution, giving American settlers there the right to vote. Queen Liliuokalani, who took the throne in 1891, tried to decrease American power in Hawaii, but she did not succeed. Rebels—natives who wanted the United States to annex Hawaii—invited an American warship to anchor in Hawaii, and helped Americans take over the government of Hawaii in 1893. However, due to opposition in the United States, Hawaii did not formally became a United States territory until 1900. Hawaii became the nation's fiftieth state in 1959.

The Society Islands went to France. France first declared Tahiti and the other islands protectorates in

1842. These protectorates depended on France for defense and gave that country partial control over their government. The islands became colonies in 1880. French Polynesia is the name applied to five groups of islands claimed by the French, including not just the Society Islands, but the Tuamotu Archipelago, the Marquesas, the Gambiers, and the Austral Islands. Today, France considers French Polynesia an overseas territory.

James Cook had claimed New Zealand in the name of his British king in 1769, but the islands did not become a colony until 1841, when British and Maori officials signed a treaty. Today, New Zealand is an independent nation that is a member of the British commonwealth.

There are now fourteen independent nations in the Pacific: Kiribati, Nauru, Papua New Guinea, Taiwan, Tuvalu, Western Samoa, Australia, Fiji, Japan, New Zealand, the Philippines, the Solomon Islands, Tonga, and Vannatu. The United States, Australia, Chile, France, Japan, New Zealand, and Great Britain still have possessions there. The native Polynesians still practice some traditional ways; their languages almost all remain in use.[15]

Cook's Legacy

James Cook was one of the greatest explorers of all time. During his three voyages, he circled the globe, becoming the first man truly to understand the geography of the South Pacific. He established contact

Captain King could not decide if gourd masks like this one were worn for protection, "purposes of mummery," or fun. Captain Cook always showed respect for the unique cultures he met.

between many South Pacific societies and Europe for the very first time. The land claims he made in the Southern Hemisphere would give Great Britain two of its most important colonies, Australia and New Zealand. He also visited the extremes of the earth, crossing both the Antarctic and the Arctic circles. But he was far more than a geographer and an explorer. He also deserves recognition as a scientist who studied the places he went and people he met; as a cartographer who made amazingly accurate maps; and as an able leader, whose crews trusted him as he led them on dangerous missions to mysterious places.

Cook showed great respect for the native people he met, although the British often regarded them as uncivilized. They were objects of curiosity but not worth a great deal of scholarly attention. The artifacts Cook collected went to what one historian called the British Museum's "rag-and-bone" department.[16] Scientists were much more interested in "natural curiosities," items from nature, than manmade artifacts.

Today, monuments have been erected to Cook's memory all over the world. They can be found in Hawaii, Tahiti, and in many other places in Polynesia. The Australian and New Zealand governments have also marked some of the places he visited.

A replica of Cook's ship *Endeavour* also sails the oceans today.[17] Crowds turn out to greet it whenever it arrives at a harbor. James Cook's voyages clearly continue to spark the imaginations and curiosity of people around the world.

Timeline

ca. **1000**—Oceania—including Polynesia, Melanesia, and Micronesia—is completely settled; Settlers have reached the South Pacific islands by making long, dangerous voyages in canoes.

1492—Christopher Columbus becomes the first European explorer of his day to reach the New World, making landfall in the Caribbean; He believes he has reached the Orient; In the decades that follow, Spain and other European powers will launch many more exploring expeditions.

1497—Vasco da Gama sails on behalf of Portugal around Africa to India.

1519 –1522 Ferdinand Magellan is the commander of the first expedition known to circumnavigate the world.

1578—Great Britain sends explorer Francis Drake to search for the fabled southern continent of Terra Australis.

1627—The Dutch reach the south coast of Australia, which they call New Holland.

1728—James Cook is born on October 27 in Marton-in-Cleveland, England.

ca. **1744**—Cook leaves home to go to work in the nearby town of Staithes for a storekeeper.

1746—Cook moves to the port of Whitby, where he apprentices himself to the owner of a coal ship and begins a life of voyaging.

1755—Cook is offered command of a coal ship but joins the British Navy instead.

1759—As master of a Navy ship, Cook charts Canada's St. Lawrence River.

1762—Cook returns to England from Canada and marries Elizabeth Batts; He then returns to Canada with the Navy.

1767—Alexander Dalrymple publishes a book in which he states his firm belief that the Terra Australis exists.

1768 –1771—Cook makes his first voyage to the South Pacific, carrying a team of scientists to Tahiti to observe a transit of Venus; Heading home, he investigates both New Zealand and Australia.

1772 –1775—On a second voyage of exploration, James Cook continues to search for the fabled southern continent, heading farther south than any explorer to that time.

1776—Cook begins his third voyage of exploration, for the primary purpose of searching for the Northwest Passage.

1778—On January 18, James Cook becomes the first European explorer known to have seen Hawaii, when he sights two of its islands from his ship; After staying there for a short time, he continues on to the Pacific Northwest.

1779—Having returned to Hawaii, Cook is killed by natives, on February 14; His men continue the expedition.

Chapter Notes

Chapter 1. James Cook "Discovers" Hawaii

1. James Cook, *Voyages of Discovery* (Chicago: Academy Chicago Publishers, 1993), p. 346.

2. Ibid.

3. James Cook, *The Journals of Captain James Cook* (Cambridge, England: Cambridge University Press, 1955–1967), vol. 3, p. 449.

4. Cook, *Voyages,* p. 349.

5. J. C. Beaglehole, *The Life of Captain James Cook* (Stanford, Calif.: Stanford University Press, 1974), p. 576.

6. Cook, *Voyages,* p. 350.

7. Cook, *Journals,* vol. 1, p. 285.

Chapter 2. The South Pacific Before Cook's Arrival

1. Peter Bellwood, *The Polynesians: Prehistory of an Island People,* Rev. ed. (London: Thames and Hudson, 1987), pp. 8–9.

2. Ibid., p. 7.

3. David Lewis, *We, The Navigators* (Canberra: Australian National University Press, 1972), passim.

4. T. Gladwin, *East Is a Big Bird* (Cambridge, Mass.: Harvard University Press, 1970), p. 129.

5. Brian Durrans, "Ancient Pacific Voyaging: Cook's Views and the Development of Interpretation," *Captain Cook and the South Pacific* (London: British Museum Publications Ltd for British Museum and the British Library Board, 1979), p. 137.

6. Ibid., p. 143.

7. James Cook, *The Journals of Captain James Cook* (Cambridge, England: Cambridge University Press, 1955–1967), vol. 1, p. 154.

8. J. A. Moerenhout, *Voyages aux Iles du Grand Ocean* (Paris, n.p., 1837), passim.

9. R. C. Green, "Sites with Lapita Pottery: Importing and Voyaging," *Mankind,* vol. 9, 1973, p. 256.

10. Bellwood, p. 14.

11. Ibid., pp. 23, 28.

12. Ibid., pp. 26–27.

13. Dorota Czarkowska Starzecka, "The Society Islands," *Cook's Voyages and the Peoples of the Pacific,* ed. Hugh Cobbe (London: British Museum Publications Ltd for the Trustees of the British Museum and the British Library Board, 1979), p. 48.

14. Dorota Czarkowska Starzecka, "Hawaii," *Cook's Voyages and the Peoples of the Pacific,* ed. Hugh Cobbe (London: British Museum Publications Ltd for the Trustees of the British Museum and the British Library Board, 1979), pp. 123ff.

15. Starzecka, "The Society Islands," pp. 47–60.

16. Dorota Czarkowska Starzecka, "New Zealand," *Cook's Voyages and the Peoples of the Pacific,* ed. Hugh Cobbe (London: British Museum Publications Ltd for the Trustees of the British Museum and the British Library Board, 1979), pp. 71–88.

Chapter 3. Early Explorers of the Pacific

1. Piers Pennington, *The Great Explorers* (London: Bloomsbury Books, 1989), p. 229.

2. Polynesian Voyaging Society, "Hawai'iloa and the Discovery of Hawaii," *Voyaging Traditions*, n.d., <http://leahi.kcc.hawaii.edu/org/pvs/traditionsloa.html> (January 29, 2001).

3. William H. Goetzmann, *New Lands, New Men* (New York: Viking, 1986), p. 8.

4. Angus Konstam, *Historical Atlas of Exploration* (New York: Benchmark Books, 2000), p. 12.

5. Pennington, p. 231.

6. Ibid., pp. 58–63.

7. Hugh Cobbe, "The Voyages and Their Background," *Cook's Voyages and the Peoples of the Pacific,* ed. Hugh Cobbe (London: British Museum Publications Ltd for the Trustees of the British Museum and the British Library Board, 1979), p. 13.

8. Ibid.

9. Alexander Dalrymple, *An account of the discoveries made in the South Pacifick previous to 1764* (London, n.p., 1767), p. 88.

10. Alexander Dalrymple, *A Collection of Voyages Chiefly in the Southern Atlantick Ocean* (London: n.p., 1772), p. 6.

Chapter 4. James Cook's Early Life

1. J. C. Beaglehole, *The Life of Captain James Cook* (Stanford, Calif.: Stanford University Press, 1974), pp. 1–5.

2. Alistair MacLean, *Captain Cook* (Garden City, N.Y.: Doubleday, 1972), p. 15.

3. Ibid., p. 16.

4. Hugh Cobbe, "The Voyages and their Background," *Cook's Voyages and the Peoples of the Pacific,* ed. Hugh Cobbe (London: British Museum Publications Ltd for the Trustees of the British Museum and the British Library Board, 1979), p. 22.

5. Beaglehole, p. 15.

6. Piers Pennington, *The Great Explorers* (London: Bloomsbury Books, 1989), p. 253.

Chapter 5. Cook's First Voyage of Exploration

1. William H. Goetzmann, *New Lands, New Men* (New York: Viking, 1986), p. 1.

2. Daniel J. Boorstin, The Discoverers (New York: Random House, 1983), p. 280.

3. Goetzmann, p. 28.

4. Piers Pennington, *The Great Explorers* (London: Bloomsbury Books, 1989), p. 253.

5. J. C. Beaglehole, *The Life of Captain James Cook* (Stanford, Calif.: Stanford University Press, 1974), p. 125.

6. Boorstin, p. 280.

7. Royal Society, *Philosophical Transactions,* vol. 57, 1767, p. 215.

8. Beaglehole, p. 129.

9. Ibid., pp. 134–140.

10. Ibid., p. 141.

11. Hugh Cobbe, "The Voyages and their Background," *Cook's Voyages and the Peoples of the Pacific,* ed. Hugh Cobbe (London: British Museum Publications Ltd for the Trustees of the British Museum and the British Library Board, 1979), p. 27.

12. David Mackay, *In the Wake of Cook: Exploration, Science, and Empire 1780–1801* (London: Croom Helm, 1985), p. 16.

13. James Cook, *The Journals of Captain James Cook* (Cambridge, England: Cambridge University Press, 1955–1967), vol. 1, p. 75.

14. Cobbe, p. 27.

15. Cook, p. cclxxx

16. Ibid., p. cclxxxiii.

17. Ibid., p. 66.

18. Pennington, p. 254.

19. Cook, p. 172.

20. Cobbe, p. 28.

21. J. C. Beaglehole, ed., *The Voyage of the Endeavour, Journals of Captain James Cook on his Voyages of Discovery,* vol. 1 (Cambridge and London: The Hakluyt Society, 1955), p. 75.

22. Dorota Czarkowska Starzecka, *Cook's Voyages and the Peoples of the Pacific,* ed. Hugh Cobbe (London: British Museum Publications Ltd for the Trustees of the British Museum and the British Library Board, 1979), p. 68.

23. Cobbe, pp. 28–29.

24. Ibid., p. 12.

25. Goetzmann, p. 40.

26. Cook, p. 399.

27. Beaglehole, p. 238.

28. Cobbe, p. 34.

29. "Cook's Journal: Queensland Coast (1770)," n.d., <http://pacific.vita.org/pacific/cook/jclqld.htm> (January 29, 2001).

30. Beaglehole, p. 276.

31. Ibid.

32. Cobbe, p. 34.

Chapter 6. Cook's Second Voyage, 1772–1775

1. Hugh Cobbe, "The Voyages and their Background," *Cook's Voyages and the Peoples of the Pacific*, ed. Hugh Cobbe (London: British Museum Publications Ltd for the Trustees of the British Museum and the British Library Board, 1979), p. 34.

2. Adrienne L. Kaeppler, "Tracing the History of Hawaiian Cook Voyage Artefacts in the Museum of Mankind," *Captain Cook and the South Pacific* (London: British Museum Publications Ltd for the Trustees of the British Museum and the British Library Board, 1979), p. 167.

3. J. C. Beaglehole, *The Life of Captain James Cook* (Stanford, Calif.: Stanford University Press, 1974), p. 294.

4. Ibid., p. 295.

5. Ibid., p. 296.

6. Cobbe, p. 34.

7. Beaglehole, p. 288.

8. Cobbe, p. 43.

9. Piers Pennington, *The Great Explorers* (London: Bloomsbury Books, 1989), p. 256.

10. James Cook, *The Journals of Captain James Cook* (Cambridge, England: Cambridge University Press, 1955–1967), vol. 2, p. 75.

11. Pennington, p. 257.

12. James Cook, *A Voyage towards the South Pole and round the world, performed in His Majesty's Ships the* Resolution *and* Adventure, *in the Years 1772, 1773, 1774, and 1775* (Dublin, n.p., 1784), p. iv.

13. William H. Goetzmann, *New Lands, New Men* (New York: Viking, 1986), p. 46.

14. "Cook's Journal, September 1773," *Captain Cook Study Unit*, 2001, <http://freespace.virgin.net/chris.jones/ccsuj2.html> (January 29, 2001).

15. Cobbe, p. 37.

16. Dorota Czarkowska Starzecka, *Cook's Voyages and the Peoples of the Pacific*, ed. Hugh Cobbe (London: British Museum

Publications Ltd for the Trustees of the British Museum and the British Library Board, 1979), p. 69.

17. Pennington, p. 257.

18. Cook, *Journals,* p. 322.

19. Ibid., p. 353.

20. Cobbe, p. 37.

21. "Cook's Journal, March 1774," *Captain Cook Study Unit,* 2001, <http://freespace.virgin.net/chris.jones/ccsuj4.html> (January 29, 2001).

22. Beaglehole, p. 442.

23. David Mackay, *In the Wake of Cook: Exploration, Science, and Empire 1780–1801* (London: Croom Helm, 1985), p. 29.

24. Cook, *Journals,* p. 643.

25. Beaglehole, p. 451.

26. Ibid., p. 473.

Chapter 7. Cook's Third Voyage, 1776–1779

1. J. C. Beaglehole, *The Life of Captain James Cook* (Stanford, Calif.: Stanford University Press, 1974), p. 505.

2. James Cook, *The Journals of Captain James Cook* (Cambridge, England: Cambridge University Press, 1955–1967), vol. 3, p. 1512.

3. Beaglehole, p. 515.

4. Ibid., p. 517.

5. James Cook, *Voyages of Discovery* (Chicago: Academy Chicago Publishers, 1993), p. 260.

6. Beaglehole, p. 549.

7. Cook, *Journals,* vol. 3, pp. 231–232.

8. Beaglehole, p. 560.

9. Cook, *Journals,* vol. 3, p. 229.

10. Cook, *Voyages,* p. 333.

11. Ibid.

12. Hugh Cobbe, ed., *Cook's Voyages and the Peoples of the Pacific* (London: British Museum Publications Ltd for the Trustees of the British Museum and the British Library Board, 1979), p. 42.

13. Cook, *Journals,* vol. 3, p. 285.

14. Cobbe, p. 42.

15. J.C.H. King, "The Nootka of Vancouver Island," *Cook's Voyages and the Peoples of the Pacific,* ed. Hugh Cobbe (London: British Museum Publications Ltd for the Trustees of the British Museum and the British Library Board, 1979), p. 89.

16. "The first British Ship on the NW Coast," *Bruce@hallman. org,* n.d., <http://www.hallman.org/indian/cook.html> (January 29, 2001).

17. Cook, *Voyages,* p. 374.

18. Cook, *Journals,* vol. 3, p. 375.

19. Beaglehole, p. 608.

20. Cobbe, p. 44.

21. Marshall Sahlins, *How "Natives" Think: About Captain Cook, for Example* (Chicago: University of Chicago Press, 1995), pp. 21, 22.

22. Dorota Czarkowska Starzecka, "Hawaii," *Cook's Voyages and the Peoples of the Pacific,* ed. Hugh Cobbe (London: British Museum Publications Ltd for the Trustees of the British Museum and the British Library Board, 1979), p. 123.

23. Sahlins, p. 78.

24. Ibid., p. 80.

25. John Ledyard, *John Ledyard's Journal of Captain Cook's Last Voyage,* ed. James Kenneth Munford (Corvallis: Oregon State University Press, 1963), p. 141.

26. Heinrich Zimmerman, *The Third Voyage of Captain Cook* (Fairfield, Wash.: Ye Galleon Press, 1988), p. 103.

27. Gananath Obeyeskere, *The Apotheosis of Captain Cook: European Mythmaking in the Pacific* (Princeton, N.J.: Princeton University Press, 1992).

28. Starzecka, p. 125.

29. Cobbe, p. 45.

30. David Mackay, *In the Wake of Cook: Exploration, Science, and Empire 1780–1801* (London: Croom Helm, 1985), p. 57.

31. Ibid., p. 59.

32. Beaglehole, p. 692.

33. Ibid., p. 695.

Chapter 8. Cook's Impact

1. William H. Goetzmann, *New Lands, New Men* (New York: Viking, 1986), p. 276.

2. Helen Wallis, "Conclusion," *Cook's Voyages and the Peoples of the Pacific,* ed. Hugh Cobbe (London: British Museum Publications Ltd for the Trustees of the British Museum and the British Library Board, 1979), p. 130.

3. Ibid., p. 130.

4. Ibid., p. 132.

5. Peter Bellwood, *The Polynesians: Prehistory of an Island People,* Rev. ed. (London: Thames & Hudson, 1978), p. 15.

6. Wallis, p. 134.

7. David Mackay, *In the Wake of Cook: Exploration, Science, and Empire 1780-1801* (London: Croom Helm, 1985), Preface.

8. Marshall Sahlins, *How "Natives" Think About Captain Cook, For Example* (Chicago: University of Chicago Press, 1995), p. 87.

9. Ibid., p. 98.

10. Bellwood, p. 15.

11. Ibid.

12. Ibid.

13. Wallis, p. 142.

14. Bellwood, p. 16.

15. Ibid., p. 23.

16. H. J. Braunholtz, "Ethnography Since Sloane," *Sir Hans Sloane and Ethnography* (London, 1973), p. 45.

17. HM Bark Endeavour Foundation, *Endeavour*, n.d., <http://www.barkendeavour.com.au> (September 7, 2001).

Further Reading

Books

Alter, Judy. *Extraordinary Explorers and Adventurers.* Chicago: Children's Press, 2001.

Blumberg, Rhoda. *Remarkable Voyages of Captain Cook.* New York: Bradbury Press, 1991.

Captain Cook and His Exploration of the Pacific. Hauppage, N.Y.: Barron's Educational Series, Inc., 1998.

Dunford, Betty, and Reilly Ridgell. *Pacific Neighbors: The Islands of Micronesia, Melanesia, and Polynesia.* Honolulu, Hawaii: The Bess Press, 1997.

Konstam, Angus. *Historical Atlas of Exploration, 1492–1600.* New York: Checkmark Books, 2000.

The Story of Captain Cook. New York: Penguin Putnam, Inc., 1991.

Internet Addresses

Excelsior Information Systems Ltd. "Captain Cook Birthplace Museum." *aboutbritain.* 1999-2000. <http://www.aboutbritain .com/captaincookbirthplacemuseum.htm>.

Mariners' Museum. *James Cook Web page.* August 1997. <http://www.mariner.org/age/cook.html>.

Thinkquest. "Biography: James Cook." *Epic Voyages: Uncovering the World.* n.d. <http://library.thinkquest.org/C004237/ english/iecook.html>.

Index